The Funny Thing

about Grief

Brittany -
Thank you for sharing
your story and Faith!
You help others in grief
not feel alone and
have given me strength
to tell my story!
Love Kar

ANDREW JOHN STIFTER
1981–2016

Life is short but sweet for certain.
— Dave Matthews Band

The Funny Thing about Grief

A Young Widow's Journey
to Find Joy through Tragedy

Katie Stifter

BEAVER'S POND
PRESS

The Funny Thing about Grief © 2020 by Katie Stifter

Edited by Angela Wiechmann
Book design and typesetting by Dan Pitts
Cover photo by Ryan O'Conner
Managing Editor: Laurie Buss Herrmann

ISBN 13: 978-1-64343-957-0
Library of Congress Catalog Number: 2019905608
Printed in the United States of America
First Printing: 2020
24 23 22 21 20   5 4 3 2 1

BEAVER'S POND
PRESS

939 Seventh Street West
Saint Paul, MN 55102
(952) 829-8818
www.BeaversPondPress.com

To order, visit www.ItascaBooks.com or call (800) 901-3480 ext. 118.
Reseller discounts available.

Contact the author at www.thewickedwidow.com or on Facebook
(@katiethewickedwidow) or on Instagram (@katiethewickedwidow)
for school visits, speaking engagements, book club discussions,
and interviews.

This book is dedicated to Andy.

May I continue to tell his story,
keep his memory
forever on my lips, in my heart,
until our souls are reunited.
Until that day comes, I will
continue to live!
Oh, and laugh!

Contents

Let's Get to Know the Crazy Widow

My name is Katie. I'm just an average girl. I grew up in a small town. I had a pretty normal childhood, with two loving parents and two older brothers. Went to college, met a boy, fell in love, and started a family.

Oh yeah. I should mention one more little thing: my husband died, leaving me a thirty-five-year-old pregnant widow with two small children.

As I reflect on who I am, I can see the role humor has played in my life. It's always been there. I just didn't realize its importance until now.

Growing up, I had to have a sense of humor to survive in our house. There was and still is a lot of jabbing and teasing. My family would probably say I was overly sensitive to it. I would run screaming into my room if I lost Monopoly. But to each their own, right?

My family was not perfect by any means, but there was always laughter in the house. That's where I learned to use laughter as a coping mechanism. Even in what I thought were the worst of times, we would always laugh at something or someone and get through life together.

That still rings true for us today. I mean, for God's sake—my dad and I play a game of "Whose Life Is Worse?" (I always win.) If that's not making lemonade out of lemons, I don't know what is. But more about that later.

I love laughing. I have one of those embarrassing laughs, one a kind person might may say is *infectious*. Many people can pick me out just by hearing my laugh.

My late husband, Andy, would always tease me about my laugh. You know, "Stop cackling so loud" or "You may have the loudest laugh I have ever heard." Sweet things like that. So, me being me, I decided to change the sound of my laugh one day. Let's just say that within an hour, he was begging me to go back to my real laugh.

It's one of my kids' favorite stories. "Hey, Mom—remember when you changed your laugh for a day?" Those are the kinds of moments I want my kids to remember when they think of me. I love to be happy. I love making people happy. And I love laughing.

I also love God. (*Uh . . . she's talking about God. I thought this book was about humor and grief.*)

Just so we're clear on this, if you don't want to hear someone get preachy, then you came to the right spot. I do talk about God in this book. But not because I want to preach to you or convert you in any way. Rather, I talk about God simply because he's part of my story. As for you and your story, well, you have to get there on your own.

Again, I'm not here to preach. But this is who I am. You chose to read my book. God's in it.

So deal.

I'm a cradle Catholic. Growing up, I went to church every Sunday. Still do. But if I can be real here, I have to admit I didn't have a relationship with God until Andy passed away. (Psst . . . don't tell my mom.)

Before, I went through the motions. I prayed when things were tough. But I didn't know God until I realized I was nothing without him.

We had many battles, God and I, throughout my first year. When I say "battles," I mainly mean I battled him. He didn't battle me. In fact, he never left my side.

I have no idea how someone could be at their lowest point, experiencing the ultimate worst that life can throw at them, without faith. Without God.

Side note: Some people *think* they've been at their lowest. They haven't. Rather, you *know* when you're there. Me, I can honestly say I know. I get bragging rights. (I know, I know—sick widow humor.) Maybe you know you've been there too. Or maybe you know you're there right now.

The point is, at the end of most days during my lowest time, God was *all* I had.

Now, some might argue, "Oh, but you had your family" and "Oh, but you needed to live for your children." But when you're so deep in the thick of grief, you can't even see straight or think straight. All you have is God by your side.

And he will never leave you.

Take what you want from this. But for me, a true and real relationship with God is the only reason I'm here writing this book.

OK, widow-talking-about-God moment over.

Just so we're up to speed, I'm an average lady who happens to be a widow with an annoying laugh and who loves Jesus.

Let's get this thing started.

Chapter 1

UMM, BUT GRIEF *ISN'T* FUNNY

———————

You might have stared at the title of this book, scratching your head. *The Funny Thing about Grief*? Grief isn't funny, is it? Humor and grief don't seem to fit together, do they?

They do, actually. Honestly, laughter has helped me throughout my grief journey. This book is the story of how I survived my worst nightmare and came out laughing and crying—and laughing and crying—but most importantly *living*.

The funny thing about grief (if there is something funny about it) is that no matter how deep you're in it and no matter how much you feel a part of you has died with your loved one, life keeps moving. Through all the pain, there is still life, love, and laughter.

The phrase "Laughter is the best medicine" comes to mind. It rings so true to me. It almost feels like my own personal mantra. As you get to know me and Andy throughout this journey, you'll understand it more clearly.

I believe Andy continues to talk to me and bring laughter into my life, especially at the hardest moments. (I know, I know—crazy widow lady talks to her dead husband.) But here's an example.

On the way to Andy's funeral, I was feeling so desperate and brokenhearted. As I was walking my sad little self to the car, I slipped on some ice and fell headfirst into my car window.

"Really, God?" I said out loud.

Then I turned and looked in the car. It was filled with the laughing, smiling faces of my mom and kids. Instantly, I burst out laughing.

I've also found it very helpful to tell funny stories about Andy—including his death. (I told you—this is sick widow humor.) One time, my daughter and I discussed how Daddy's paddleboard ended up at a police auction.

"Oh yeah—I'm sure that was a great auction item," she remarked with a smirk on her face. "Hey, who wants to buy this paddleboard that a guy died on?" (Good Lord, that poor girl has my same sick humor. Look out, world.)

She and I looked at each other and laughed so hard our stomachs hurt. But once I caught my breath, I immediately explained that even though *we* could laugh with each other about that, it was maybe not an appropriate joke to tell others. That would definitely make an outsider cringe or give us the crazy eyes.

But come on—this life, this experience of grief, is so intense and so sad that the only thing left to do is laugh. This is how Andy's death has bonded us as a family. This is how our laughter, in the end, has helped heal us.

Now, before we go any further, let me clear up a few things.

One, I'm not saying humor is a one-size-fits-all approach to grief. Everyone processes grief so differently. There is no "correct" way. We are all so unique, from our upbringing and culture to our personality and gender. The nature of how our loved one passed also affects how we grieve.

Watching my parents, in-laws, siblings, and friends after Andy's death, I am positive there is no one way to grieve. You've probably witnessed it too, even among people from the same family. Some people keep themselves busy. Some cry uncontrollably. Some don't talk. Some avoid their feelings. The list could go on.

The point is, just because humor works for me doesn't mean it will work for you. Maybe it's not your go-to coping strategy. You must grieve in your own way and on your own terms. However, be cautious if you find yourself grieving in an unhealthy manner.

Two, I'm not saying that laughter and humor will make the pain of grief magically disappear. By laughing after I hit my head on the car window, did I instantly "get over" the fact that I was heading to my husband's funeral as a thirty-five-year-old widow with two kids and one on the way? Hell, no!

Laughter doesn't solve life's problems or bring a loved one back. But it does bring life back into your soul and give you a glimmer of hope—even for just a brief moment—that joy will return and that life is worth living.

Three, by no means will I ever downplay the pain of grief in this book. Grief is a heart-wrenching, crying-on-your-bathroom-floor-making-noises-you-don't-even-recognize, wouldn't-wish-this-on-your-worst-enemy kind of pain. Believe me—my ugly-cry face with running mascara is proof.

There are days and moments when out of nowhere, grief's dark power overcomes me, and even laughter can't keep it at bay. Grief will always be there, lurking, waiting to suck me in.

But through my grief and pain, I now understand that happiness is a choice. It's not a gift we are given or a privilege bestowed on us.

Each morning, we get to choose our life perspective. We get to choose how we face each day and how we handle each obstacle thrown our way. We can choose to be happy, let the little things go, forgive others, and laugh.

This knowledge has given me power back over my grief. Grief does not *control* me. It may *overcome* me sometimes, but I can take control over it. That's because in the end, I will always choose happiness. Always.

I feel compelled to help others choose happiness too, to smile, to be happy, and to laugh. You too can choose happiness for your deceased loved one and your family, but most importantly, for the gift of life God has given you! Despite the pain.

Four, when I talk about humor and grief, I'm not reinventing the wheel or stating anything that hasn't already been researched or studied. There's been countless research on laughter and the human body. I could cite a bunch of boring stats and quotes, but I won't. (Mainly because I'm a widow with three kids. I have no time for all those footnotes.)

Also, let's not forget the numerous times laughter is mentioned in the Bible. For example, "Laughter can conceal the heavy heart, but when laughter ends, the grief remains" (Proverbs 14:13).

Do your own research if you don't believe the crazy ranting widow. Otherwise, just take it from me: laughter can help boost your immune system, concentration, brain function, and memory. Simply put, laughter is good for the body and soul.

That's why it's so important during times of grief. Let's face it—we tend not to take great care of ourselves when we face tragedy. I kindly call it the "grief diet." This can involve, but is not limited to, the following behavior: not eating enough or eating too much, not sleeping enough or sleeping too much, not exercising, uncontrolled stress, anxiety, deep sadness, depression. And of course, the ugly-cry face that happens in Target when you're trying to buy freakin' new underwear for your kids because all the other things listed above leave you too exhausted to do laundry.

I've noticed that the grief diet also goes hand in hand with the downward spiral lovingly known as "widow brain." Ask my daughter. I once dropped her off at the wrong spot for basketball practice. If the grief diet and widow brain hadn't done me in, the looks I got from my preteen would have. (Love you, Grace! Don't be mad I wrote that into my story.)

When you're consumed with the grief diet and widow brain, laughter can give you a feeling of "normal"—even if for just a brief moment. But that moment is worth it when you're literally counting the seconds in the day to be over.

Five, one of my goals with this book is to use humor to help break through some taboos. (Yes, this sick widow humor has a purpose.)

In Western society, we are not taught about death, how to cope with it, or how to help others. No one ever knows what to say or how to help a grieving person. It's mind-blowing. Maybe *flabbergasting* is a better word. After all, everyone—I mean, *everyone*—experiences the passing of a loved one.

This taboo, I have learned, comes from fear. Some people don't talk about death because they fear they'll make the grieving person uncomfortable. Frankly, many people are more afraid the grieving person will make *them* uncomfortable. They just hope we "get over it." And quickly.

And under it all, most people fear their own mortality and that of their loved ones. Death, especially a tragic one like Andy's, makes people pause, look at their own life, and think, *What if that happened to me?* I became a living representation that any one of us may suddenly lose someone we love.

But that thought is so disturbing, so painful, that most people must quickly get rid of it. They turn away from the grieving person and tell themselves, *No, no—that could never happen to me.*

Just like grief is taboo for many people, so is mental health, and they walk side by side. Grief can be linked to a variety of mental-health issues that can be expressed in a variety of ways.

Many who know me, for instance, would be shocked to learn that I suffer from depression and anxiety. Throughout my life, I've always been an anxious person, and anxiety runs in my family. Up until Andy's passing, I was able to use coping strategies during times of stress.

But his death intensified these predispositions, sending me into a tailspin of sadness and anxiety that others couldn't always see. I'm proof that mental health doesn't look the same in all people. Just because someone wears a smile doesn't mean sadness isn't behind it.

We need to stop shying away from mental-health issues, just as we need to stop shying away from grief. The more we talk about these so-called elephants in the room (or widows in the room), the more we can love and support each other. And perhaps humor is one way to break the ice.

Oh, by the way—countless reliable articles and studies have also shown how laughter helps those who struggle with mental health.

I know the "Big Guy" gave me the gift of humor and joy. (*Ugh. More God talk?*) I also know he gave me the gift of being able to help others. That's why I'm a school counselor by trade.

But since Andy's passing, I've felt an even deeper calling to use these gifts specifically to help those who are grieving. I hope others can look at me—someone who became a widow at thirty-five with two kids and a baby on the way—and see I'm still smiling, laughing, and living as I move forward through grief. Then maybe they might believe that they too can move forward in order to find laughter, happiness, and joy again.

OK, rambling widow soapbox moment over. Now, on to the story.

Chapter 2

THE MAN, THE MYTH, THE LEGEND

I want to pause for a minute to talk a little about Andy—who he was as a man, husband, father, and friend. A man who could fix any of our children's ailments, whether physical or mental, with one of his famous "tight squeezes."

First off, I find it very challenging to capture, in words, who Andy really was. I feel I'm doing him a disservice. But this is where Andy would step in and say, "Kate, get on with it and just write it." He was so good at bringing me back to reality and focusing on what really mattered. And I desperately miss his tight squeezes. They fixed all my problems too.

That leads me to my first description of him: he always put those he loved first. He would give you the last bite, sacrifice his needs for yours, make you laugh when you needed it most, move to a home where my commute would be shorter while his would be longer, convert to my faith and go to church every Sunday, check for intruders in the middle of the night, put up with all my emotions and give me a hug at the end of every argument, expand our family so I could live with no regrets, and love me unconditionally until the day he died.

God, I wish I could be more like that, and God, I wish I would have been more like that to him when he was alive.

But that's another funny thing about grief—you don't seem to know what's important until it's gone. But I vowed to him in the dark at his grave that I would always put those I loved first and myself second. I will do this for him, because in the end, all that matters are those we love. Period. Nothing else. (And yeah, I know it's weird to be at a cemetery in the dark, talking out loud to a dead person without being scared. But let's put a positive spin on things: "Hey, look at me—I'm not scared to be in a cemetery alone in the dark anymore!")

Andy was, seriously still is, and always will be the funniest person I have ever met. To know Andy was to laugh with Andy. He had so much depth to his humor.

He had goofy humor, which was probably my favorite. My last memory of the man was him dancing around in our son's Troll-hair hat, trying to get me to laugh as I ugly-pregnant-cried watching *Gilmore Girls*. How many can say that is the last memory of their loved one? I think I take the cake on that one.

The kids thrived on his goofy humor. The last months of his life, we had this ongoing goal of him perfecting "dad jokes." You know, the kind of bad jokes that make you roll your eyes and want to throw up a little bit? He took every opportunity to tell the kids as many dad jokes as possible. Being his best audience, I would always roar with laughter. The kids and I even made up a stupid song about his dad jokes. It went a little something like this: "Baaaad jokes, daaaad jokes, baaaad jokes." I hope this gives you a glimpse into our funny little life. (And don't judge me. You know you do weird things with your family too.)

These are the memories I cling to and will forever cherish. These little moments in our lives make life worth living. I want my kids to forever remember their daddy's ability to always make them laugh and embarrass himself to no end to see his kids and wife smile.

I feel so lucky to have experienced that goofy side of Andy, because most never saw it. To those who weren't close to him, he was a huge introvert. Consider yourself a lucky one if you knew that goofy side. I guess you save the best for those you love the most.

In a way, Andy's goofy side allowed me to be most like myself. Even as adults, we could act and laugh so stupid together. I hated when he would pretend he was a steamroller and roll over the top of me, when lying in bed he would hold my hands down and tickle me, or when he would pretend he was a shark and throw himself on top of me with his hands placed together like a fin. Oh, my least favorite was when he acted like a linebacker trying to tackle me as I tried to get out of the room. (I told you—we were totally a goofy couple.) Of course, my hatred of these things always ended with shrieks of laughter and annoyance all mixed together.

That might be the best way to describe our relationship: laughter mixed with a side of annoyance. I wouldn't change a second of it. God, I loved how that man annoyed me and how I equally loved to annoy him.

If you asked anyone who knew Andy, they would say he had a very sarcastic, witty, always-good-for-a-one-liner kind of humor. The kind of smart humor that you couldn't tell was a joke unless you knew him well. I think he secretly liked that.

Another funny memory comes to mind. Andy once told our neighbors—including some we didn't know that well— how I was a good first wife, but that his next marriage would definitely be for money. Andy said it so matter-of-factly right in front of me. I just laughed. I still giggle thinking about the confused look from one of the neighbors, who obviously didn't understand the humor or the man.

This humor did not die with Andy. (Sorry—that's kinda a morbid way of putting it.) His humor lives on in my little girl. She has his same snarky, sarcastic humor. Her daddy would be so proud. For God's sake, she has even been writing her own joke book, and she practices her jokes on me. I guess I will be forever an audience.

Andy was also a man of many hobbies. This is one of those things you think is cute when you're dating, but it turns so freaking annoying when you're married. Like, really, Andy? Do you have to make your own cheese? From the day we met, he always had some kind of hobby he was working on or trying to get into.

After meeting and talking to his mom, I came to find out this was not a new thing. Even as a small boy, he was a hobby man. He performed magic tricks. He was a scientist with his microscope. He had an avid love of turtles one summer (Chuck, Charlie, and Charles were their names). He was a dog rescuer and vet taking care of lost pets (Mop-Top and many other varieties of scruffy puppies). Not to mention he had an obsession with Barry Sanders. And not to knock on those who like trimming bonsai trees, but really—how did I date someone in college who wanted a bonsai tree?

But to know Andy was to embrace the weird and accept his hobbies. Here are some, but not all, of his hobbies that make me smile when I think back on them: Rubik's cube, Buddhism, cheese making, growing his own grapes and making wine, beer making, origami, snowshoe making, juicing, harmonica playing, self-taught guitar playing, cooking, marathon running, growing and making his own loofah (yes, really), brewing his own kombucha, binge-watching *Ancient Aliens* or some other history show, buying designer shoes on eBay, bread making, perfecting soup recipes, mastering the Buffalo Wild Wings challenge, Ironman training, gardening, landscaping, photography. And lastly, one I'm not so fond of anymore: paddleboarding. (Sorry. Sick widow humor again.)

The list could go on and on. If he hadn't passed away, beekeeping and raising chickens were next on his list. If I'm looking for positives, his death most likely saved numerous neighborhood children from freaking bees and chickens loose in their yards.

Some may view these hobbies as strange or weird. I found many of them super annoying—especially cheese making. Actually, in the days when Andy was still missing (stay tuned—you'll learn more later), I threw his cheese kit away. I thought, *If the man is still alive, he is not making cheese anymore.* I didn't feel bad throwing it away then, and I still don't. But this is who Andy was. As the marriage vows say, "For better, for worse, through sickness and one annoying hobby to the next, till death do us part."

This man had a zest for life and trying new things. I wish I could be that creative, challenging myself to try new things the way he did. He always liked to be *doing* and not letting life pass him by.

If he set his mind to something, he would complete it. He would do countless hours of research and plot out when he would have time to complete each hobby in his time off. As I write this, I can remember him telling his friends, "Sorry, guys—I can't hang out. I have snowshoes to make." It was in the middle of August.

When he was marathon training, a group of teenage boys drove by him and yelled out the window, "Hey, douchebag!" They then circled back to yell, "Hey, fatty!" But that didn't stop him. Now that's drive. (It was an even funnier story coming from Andy.)

I can't describe Andy without talking about his love of his children. He lived and breathed for our kids. When we brought our little Gracie home, we were living in a townhome with a steep set of stairs leading up to the entry. I remember Andy smiling and whisking Gracie upstairs—leaving me at the bottom to fend for myself.

All you mothers out there know how I felt at that moment. I had just had my first baby. I was very tender and sore from delivery. *Out with the old, in with the new*, I thought.

I then proceed to yell at him to help me up the stairs. I never let him live that down. It became one of our funny memories.

Again, I'm struggling for words that capture the deep love he had for our children. I know most parents love their kids and would do anything for them. But there was just something special about the love he had for ours. The way he would look at them, with pure love in his eyes—it's indescribable. It just had to be witnessed.

All he wanted to do (when he wasn't making cheese) was to spend time playing, coaching, hugging, and loving them. He cried when they made their first soccer goals. He listened to their little stories about their day. He wrestled them night and day. Always begged them to "have a catch" in the backyard. Required "tight squeezes" for every favor asked of him. Deep-belly laughed with them. And always tried to solve their problems with a common phrase the kids and I still laugh about: "Need a hug?"

After Andy passed away, I was adamant that my kids always feel their dad's love—especially my little Sully, who never got to meet his daddy. So from the very beginning of this journey, anytime a memory, thought, or funny story of Daddy came up, we wrote it down. I know my other children were young—only nine and six—when Andy passed away. The memories will fade, which makes capturing them so important.

I also vowed to always talk about Andy. His name will never be hushed just so we don't feel the pain of his loss. Rather, it's the opposite. We *will* talk about him so we can laugh, smile, and remember. The more you talk about *your* person, the more comfortable those around you will feel to talk about *their* loved one too. Andy is just a part of our conversation, and I want that to continue as long as we live. Of course, sometimes these stories about him produce tears. But most often, they are just daily reminders of the love he had for us—a love we will cherish.

As I pull out the book of memories we've written about him, I can't help but laugh out loud at some of the things that made Andy, well, Andy. One of my favorites that always makes us laugh is the man's inability to pick up our dog's poop without dry heaving. I mean, for God's sake—the man survived a war. He was an Iraq War army vet. I'm sure he saw and smelled the worst of the worst. Yet he could not pick up dog poop.

Oh, so many memories I cherish. He would fly the kids around in the air and act as if they were machine guns. Or whenever he passed gas, he would blame it on an infamous "barking spider."

The man wasn't all just fun and games. He always made the kids eat their veggies. He was the best homework helper. And he started a tradition of making pancakes from scratch every Saturday so it would be his thing one day when the kids would come home from college: "Dad, can you make pancakes?" And he would lovingly respond, "Sure, buddy."

There's one last characteristic you must understand to know this man. (No, Andy. It's not your rugged good looks.) It's his love of and service to his country.

When Andy was in high school, he joined the Army Reserve to help pay for his college education. Andy was a junior in college when 9/11 happened. He was called to service in Iraq, serving on the Seventy-Ninth Military Police First Platoon for a year. *Hooah.*

(I always tried to make him say "Hooah," and it drove him crazy. See? I enjoyed annoying him as well. While I'm at it, he always looked so cute in his army outfit. He hated when I said that too. Like tough army guys can't wear "outfits." It has to be "uniforms.")

I don't know how someone could come home from war and not be forever changed. It's not that Andy didn't appreciate his country before. It's just that when he returned, he had an even deeper love for his country and his fellow servicemen. It was so evident. He was so proud of what he did and how he helped protect his country. See? I told you he was selfless and always put the needs of others first.

He held Veterans Day dear to his heart and soul. He didn't care about his birthday or any other holiday, but Veterans Day was his jam. Oh Lord—the first year we were married, I forgot to wish him a happy Veterans Day, and the man held it over my head for nine long years.

As I said, it's hard to put this into words. But I hope this gives you some insight into who this man was and how laughter was always a part of his life. We, his family and friends, will keep on laughing as we think of Andy, his life, and all our memories of him.

Speaking of memories, I know you want to know how we met.

Chapter 3

The Fairy Tale

———

When Andy and I met, it was what storybooks are made of and what little girls dream of. A love story that will be told across all time and space.

I have to stop—I can literally hear Andy dry heaving from the grave.

Real story: We met at a kegger in the dirty basement of 212 Washington, where many bad decisions were made. It was the end of my freshman year of college. I was wearing a flashing Bud Lite pin. Andy came over to work his "smooth" on me. He commented on my pin, then said, "You know, I can get you to the front of the keg."

It was love at first horrible red Solo cup of Busch Light.

But I wouldn't change a thing. Because it is our story, our memory. Of course we had a funny story about how we met—funny was our thing.

He was the funniest person I had ever met. I swear he dated me so I would be his very own personal audience. He could bring me anywhere, tell a stupid joke or sneak in a stupid jab with his oh-so-dry sense of humor, and I would crack up. This was our relationship. We were always laughing.

Or maybe I should say *I* was always laughing. Me making him laugh was a little trickier. He would give me the "don't quit your day job" look for most of my jokes.

But guess who's the funny one now? *Me*! (I'm laughing as I write this joke, and I'm sure Andy is laughing right here with me. Actually, he's probably giving me the "cut it" face and gesture.)

To most people, he was Stifter. To me, he was Andy, Bubby, Droid, Shark, or any other weird nickname I'd make for him.

My love of nicknames required him to have nicknames for me as well. One time in college, I pestered him to give me a cute nickname, so he decided to call me his Little Sasquatch. Upon looking up the definition, I discovered that a Sasquatch is a "hairy, upright-walking ape-like creature that dwells in the wilderness and leaves footprints." It's Bigfoot. (I know— you can't make this stuff up, right?) Boy, did he think he was hilarious for that one. He continued to call me his Little Sasquatch for the remainder of that school year.

Mostly, though, I was his Kate, but he was also known to call me Tron, Gilly, or Dolphin. (We weren't the traditional "honey" or "baby" type couple—obviously.)

We met when we were nineteen, and we grew up together. We had a very playful relationship, always wrestling, playing, and laughing. He grounded me, and I gave him a "let's play it by ear" spirit. It just worked.

Don't get me wrong—things weren't perfect. We fought, we argued, and we yelled. But in the end, there was always love, and we laughed every second we could.

We dated all through college. We spent almost all our time together. His friends became my friends. This group of friends became my "West Side" family. Andy grew up in West Saint Paul—not to be confused with other parts of Saint Paul, because I guess there are strong views on which part of Saint Paul you live in.

Believe me, when the worst happens to you, you really learn who your friends are. And this group of people surrounded me and my children with love, support, and laughter. Andy would be so proud to call them family too, the way they came to the aid of the most precious people in his life.

This family of friends still supports me, whether it's to make sure I had changed my furnace filter (which I hadn't), threaten my daughter to never sneak out her window, wrestle with my boys, send a funny memory, or plan a get-together because they know I need a dose of West Saint Paul.

As Andy's second birthday in heaven approached, one of his best friends messaged me: "What are you doing for Andy's birthday—wanna get drunk?" My response: "Hell yeah, but only if everyone wears a tracksuit." (You see, Andy was also into wearing tracksuits for a period of time. Actually, that's what he gave our groomsmen for their groom's gift. I'm sure this doesn't surprise you by now.) So we all got together at a small bar in West Saint Paul and told stories and laughed. If I couldn't celebrate with Andy, these people were the next best thing.

I love spending time with this family because it really makes me "feel" Andy's presence. A part of him lives through them. With every high school memory and bad joke, Andy's spirit is present.

Actually, spending a day or night with these friends reminds me of Andy so much that a wave of sadness often hits me. This isn't a sadness I'd ever want to avoid, though. This is the truest compliment I could give. They keep a part of Andy alive for me.

Never be afraid to keep talking about your loved one. Yes, it hurts to think that they aren't there. But oh, to *know* you had this special person in your life, to *hold* all the memories made—it's worth every potential tear.

I know this relationship with my West Side family will continue for my lifetime. They are my people. My best advice: get these kind of people in your life. Who you spend your time with is a reflection on your character. So ditch the downers and drama, and surround yourself with people who make you better and want you to be better. You will become better because of it. (We'll talk about finding your tribe more in chapter 9.)

I better stop talking about these guys now. Some of them might get a big head. Back to the story of how Andy and I met . . .

Andy was in the Army Reserve during college, though we never had a single worry about him being deployed overseas. But then the tragedy of 9/11 occurred. Deployment now became a reality. In the days that followed, I vividly remember us crying and holding on to each other as tight as possible, as the thought of his leaving became a part of our future.

That spring, he was assigned to an army station in Wisconsin, from where he would be deployed to Iraq. He spent six or so months training and waiting for his unit to be called. I would drive to Wisconsin every weekend to see him and say goodbye, because we never knew when the day would come that he would have to leave.

Andy served for a year in Iraq. Until his death, I considered that the most challenging time I had ever gone through. The constant worry for his safety, the stress of never knowing his location, the aching heart missing him.

We communicated by snail mail. I kept all these letters and will forever cherish them. I'm not gonna lie, though: reading them makes me a little sick to my stomach. How mushy and cheesy they are. How many times we called each other "baby." (Insert barfing emoji.) We had a deep love for each other, but we were never the mushy-gushy, kissy-kissy type. Apparently, something about being separated by war does it to a person.

When Andy returned from the war, it was one of the best days of my life. I started grad school that fall, and he went on to complete his bachelor's degree, which had been put on hold while he was away.

Andy never talked about what he did and saw in Iraq. I didn't push him. I knew he would talk about it if he wanted to, because we talked about everything. Instead, he only shared stories that would make me smile. In true Andy fashion, he put laughter and me first. I'm sure part of the reason he didn't share other stories was because he didn't want to upset me or make me worry. Of course, another part was because he didn't want to reflect on the sights, sounds, and horrors of war.

When he first returned, it felt as if we were back to the old us, as if he had never left. Unfortunately, that changed. Like many who have served in wartime, Andy was diagnosed with post-traumatic stress disorder (PTSD). The PTSD made him want to retreat and be alone. It was not like my Andy.

Andy's PTSD made him withdraw at a time when I was ready for the next step in our life and our relationship. By that point, we had been dating all through college. I had stayed faithful and deeply in love with him while he served his tour in Iraq. I was ready for that next step. Actually, I had wanted to marry that man since the first day we met.

But the combination of his PTSD plus my expectations took a toll. We broke up for a short time.

Obviously, we ended up back together and married. But Andy always hated talking about our breakup. It made him feel sad. Sometimes he would get snarky and say, "Well, if you hadn't pressured me to marry you, we never would have broken up!"

I mean, really! OK, so maybe I did put a picture of an engagement ring on his computer's desktop wallpaper. And maybe I did put it on the "tile" setting, which filled the entire screen with dozens of little images of my dream ring. Is that "pressure"? I think not! (I know, I know. But c'mon. I waited an *entire year* while the man was in Iraq!)

In all reality, I'm sure thoughts of marriage and our future did play some role in our breakup. But I strongly believe that Andy's transition from war to reality was more than any person could handle without setbacks.

After our hiatus, I continued with grad school. He had graduated college, and he took a job an hour away. But then on a random Wednesday after work, there was a knock at my door. I was in my pajamas studying. (Let's be honest: I was watching TV.)

I opened the door to see my Andy down on one knee, holding a ring (yes, the one from the computer wallpaper) and a dozen white roses. With his face as white as the roses, he asked me to spend the rest of my life with him.

I of course said yes, and we kissed. I couldn't have been happier. The moment I had dreamed of since I was a little girl had finally happened. *Eek*! Now we were getting married!

We looked at each other and said, "Now what?" Social media wasn't really a thing yet, so we had to resort to telling people the old-fashioned way: in person. We set off to surprise my mom and dad with the news in person, and then we called his family.

Wedding planning went into full effect. I'm not sure Andy realized I would start planning literally the next day. But hey, it's hard to match openings at a reception venue with openings at the church. You gotta jump on that stuff right away.

At the time, all the little details about the wedding seemed so important. But the thing about loss is, you don't know what's truly important until it's gone. All that mattered was the love we had for each other—not the little pink bows I individually glued on my guests' daisy-seed-packet wedding favors. (Which, by the way, were complete with a note that read, "He loves me. He loves me not. He loves me, so we tied the knot.")

The wedding was beautiful, my groom was handsome, and I got to say "I do." I wore the pretty princess dress, even though it turned out to be literally the hottest day of the year with about 100 percent humidity.

We had so much fun celebrating with all our friends and family. One of our West Side family members broke the bathroom stall door at our venue, my brother-in-law snuck into a strip club, and we ran out of our kegs before my dad could even open his wallet. But it only added to the magic of the night. I wouldn't change it for the world. It was one of the most special days of my life.

I like to remind myself of these magical moments and days. I use them as weapons to fend off grief.

Suck it, grief, I say. *You can be so powerful that you drop me to my knees, make my children cry, and take my breath away. But you will never, never take away these wonderful memories. They are mine. And as long as I have them, I have Andy in my heart.*

These moments of triumph are so important, because grief can be such a sneaky bastard. She can come out of nowhere and stop you dead (I know—bad choice of words) in your tracks. Case in point: as I was writing this very chapter, I paused to change my baby's diaper—and suddenly I got hit with one of those "Is this really my freaking life?" moments.

How did I get here? Is he really dead? Am I really stuck changing every single diaper of a baby who will never meet his dad?

Ugh. Depressing, I know. But this is a window to widowhood. Sometimes you're able to regroup after one of those moments. Other days, you'll be a complete shit show.

The point is, give grief her moment. She deserves it. Those are honest feelings that need to be processed. But don't give grief even a second longer than she deserves.

Instead, lean in on laughter and those God-given gifts we discussed in chapter 1. Happiness is a choice, so reflect on the good in your life, remember the magical moments with your loved one, laugh and tell stories with friends, get up and change whatever you're doing, take time in prayer—whatever helps you do it!

OK, back to the story.

That spring, I finished grad school, and Andy had turned his degree in parks and recreation into a dream job at a rental-car business. (I hope you get my humor by now.) That summer was an even crazier time, for me especially. I got my first real job, got married, and moved in with Andy in our first home together. And then the really big unexpected change: I got pregnant.

Could life possibly throw any more changes at a person? (Oh yeah. I guess it can—and did. Remember? Widow at thirty-five with three kids and two dogs?)

Our Gracie was a surprise, but she was her daddy's whole world. Andy would often tell the story of how Gracie was crying in her little hospital bed, still needing to be weighed and cleaned. Andy loved to brag about how she instantly stopped crying when he put his hand on her chest.

I let him have the story. It was one of his favorites, and it shows how he was wrapped around her little, tiny finger from that first moment. In the nine years they were able to spend together, it never changed. That girl could drop a grown man to his knees with one sweet look. Andy never knew what he had coming.

"The Boy," as Andy would call him, was born a little over three years later. He is our little Ike. He came out looking like Great-Grandpa Stifter, all wrinkly and old.

Unlike Gracie, Ike is a true mama's boy. He was and still is the most empathetic and caring person I have met. In his eyes, I could do no wrong. We always laughed that he was Andy's biggest competition, as he would compliment my hair or tell me how beautiful I was before Andy could. It was a common joke that Ike was trying to move in on Andy's lady, as Ike would often wedge his way between us when Andy and I tried to hug or kiss.

Ike was also the most colicky baby ever. Andy would joke that he purposely stayed late at work those first months just to avoid Ike.

Don't get me wrong—Ike and Andy had such a special relationship. From their breakfast boy club to their wild roughhousing and "tight squeezes," that man loved his Boy, and that Boy adored his dad.

With two kids, two dogs, and a new house in a new town, we became pregnant with our third little one six years after

Ike's arrival. Andy had been very content with two children, but he knew having one more baby was very important to me. He was a very selfless man, doing whatever he could to make me happy.

Because I was thirty-five, a new title was bestowed upon my condition: geriatric pregnancy. Oh, how Andy loved that! He also couldn't wait until I weighed more than him. He was always into health and fitness and was training for an Ironman at the time, so I'm sure it wouldn't have been long before I surpassed him.

I know—wasn't he a jerk? Seriously, though, his jokes were never malicious. They were meant to make me smile. In his eyes, I was the most beautiful woman in the world, and he always made me feel this way. I mean, yes, I did punch him a lot for his stupid jokes. But I laughed with every swing.

As I have said, Andy never got to meet our baby. But he did learn the baby was a boy, which was truly a blessing. Thanks to my "advanced maternal age," I was able to find out the baby's sex via a blood test at only twelve weeks, about five weeks before Andy died. And learning the baby's sex early gave us time to decide on a name: Sullivan, or Sully for short. (No, not after the character in *Monsters, Inc.* It is a family name.)

Hear me out on this: there was a downside to having the name picked out before Andy died. If you know me, you know I love talking about baby names. (Yeah, it's weird. Don't judge.) Considering that Andy died when I was only seventeen weeks pregnant, he technically robbed me of several months of thinking of more baby names. (Yes, I can get mad him for that. He is my late husband!)

Jokes aside, it really does feel special to have shared at least that part of the pregnancy with Andy and for our son to know that his daddy helped pick his name before he died.

(Confession: I did change the middle name we agreed on.)

Wow, I just wrapped up the big moments of our lives in a few pages. Andy would be so proud.

But now I have to take some time to talk about the moments in between. The in-between is really what makes a life. These are the things I miss the most.

Having family dinner. Going to the kids' sports events. Saturday-morning breakfasts. Binge-watching our favorite TV shows. Having someone to talk to about my day. Having someone worry where you are and whether you're OK. Having someone comfort you when you are sad. Having someone to hug.

Obviously, I have other people to hug and who care about me. But it's not the same. When you lose a spouse, there is such an overwhelming feeling of loneliness.

This is my biggest battle: missing the in-between, the normal, the boring days when we were just a family. In fact, now I struggle with what it means to be a family without one of the biggest pieces—my best friend and father to my children. It just doesn't seem like a "family" anymore.

The hard thing is, there's no fix for this. While laughter and humor can help, they can't change the situation and bring him back. So it's all about perspective. As I said and will continue to say, I choose happiness.

You might be wondering if the in-between moments included some not-so-fun stuff. Absolutely! When a loved one dies, there's definitely a tendency to idealize them. Have I done this? Again, absolutely!

Why do we do this? Is it healthy? Sorry. I don't have a research-based answer for this. I'm sure there is one, but there's no time to dig around for it, thanks to the countless pets and children running around my house.

So here's my nonscientific, I'm-a-widow-so-I-must-be-right answer instead: Why would I want to think of all the not-good things about our marriage and life? Why would I focus my limited energy on what was wrong? I don't want to add more sadness to my already huge pile.

I focus on the positives because my children were young when they lost their dad. If I am honest—and this stings a lot—I know they will eventually have a limited memory of him. Or in Sully's case, no memory at all. It is my job, then, as their mother to keep Andy's memory alive. And I want them to have memories of their happy, funny, loving, silly daddy.

That's not to say that I've put him on a pedestal no other person can live up to or surpass. There will never be another Andy. But that doesn't mean there can't or won't be someone equally special who comes into my life and makes me happy. Overly idealizing your loved one can inhibit your ability to move forward on a different path.

So yeah, I've painted a pretty picture of who Andy was and what our relationship was like. But I think I've sprinkled in some not-so-rosy honesty too. As I said before, the man sometimes drove me crazy. And as impossible as this sounds, because I'm a bright ray of sunshine, I drove him insane too.

Have you ever looked at your spouse and thought, *Why do I even let you touch me?* Of course you have, and I did too. Andy and I disagreed, fought, and screamed, and one of us may have thrown a box of donuts at the other. (Only a dumb man eats a pregnant woman's donuts.)

Andy and I were married for ten years and had known each other for almost sixteen years. But we were different people with different personalities and different views about life. He was an introvert, a thinker. He liked to be on time, always had a daily plan, was cool and collected, and spent money wisely. I, on the other hand, am a huge extrovert, a feeler. I never have a plan for the day, am never on time, am spunky and feisty, and am a shopper. So of course we fought and drove each other crazy.

But in the end, there was always the commitment we made to each other, and there was always, always love. We may have had our differences, but our core values—family and faith— were in sync.

So just as I choose happiness each day, I choose to keep the good memories about Andy and our relationship in the forefront of my memory—for me as well as for my kids. There's a place for the not-so-good memories too, but I choose to laugh at those. I mean, the man grew his own loofahs.

Enough said.

Chapter 4

PRELUDE TO THE NIGHTMARE

I want to prepare you. We are nearing the part of the book I've been dreading the most. My journey through hell and back.

It's easy to talk about Andy and our relationship but not so easy to reflect upon the darkest time in my life. Honestly, it's something I try to avoid, even if I know that's not the healthiest of choices.

I wish I could forget this period in my life, but its moments and memories are forever etched in my brain. They will replay in my mind for the rest of my life, like a song I can't get out of my head.

Then again, I truly believe your brain blocks certain pieces of the memories to protect you during and after trauma. You can only handle so much at a time.

As I write this, it's been over a year. My brain must be telling me I'm healing, because those sneaky memories are making their way back. Sometimes it can be as simple as putting on my winter boots and remembering that I wore them when we were searching for Andy. Or maybe it's a change in the weather, a song on the radio, even a dead ladybug on my kitchen windowsill. Who knew a dead ladybug could bring a grown woman to her knees in tears? Grief is a mysterious broad. (I will get to the ladybug later.)

What I'm trying to say is, the next few chapters will be a journey as I process the memories and feelings my brain and I have avoided for a year. (Wish me luck!) I know this journey will be soul-healing for me, but I hope it'll also be a journey for you, as readers. I hope you get some takeaways from my memories, experiences, and random thoughts.

As I contemplated how to write these next chapters, I prayed and spent some time reading God's word. (Yep, here's that widow-talking-about-God stuff again.) I was directed to a passage in Psalms 102, which is a prayer of the afflicted person. I was like, "Bingo. Was this written about me?" There is a passage that really describes my pain: "My heart is withered, dried up like grass, too wasted to eat my food. From my loud groaning, I become skin and bones."

Yuck, I know. Totally depressing. But this was my grief. This is what the next chapters are about.

If you have experienced a similar death in your life, then you know my pain. The pain is so deep, and the ache is so strong, that you really—I mean *really, really*—don't know if you can carry on.

But you do, somehow. Just as God's word continues on.

In fact, the very next psalm speaks to what I mentioned before in chapter 1, that we must lean in on God and the gifts he has given us: "Bless the LORD, oh my soul; and do not forget all his gifts, who pardons all your sins, and heals all your ills, who redeems your life from the pit, and crowns you with mercy and compassion, who fills your days with good things."

I particularly like the description of delivering us from the "pit." That is exactly how I felt, that my life was in a dark pit with no way out. But God always shines a light and extends a hand. If we lean in on his chest, we can hear his heartbeat: "I love you, I love you, I love you."

Again, I just wanted to prepare you. Get ready, because my life's nightmare is about to start.

Chapter 5

THE NIGHTMARE:
THE FIRST TWENTY-FOUR HOURS

————————————

It happened two days after Thanksgiving.

It was a normal Saturday in our home. The weather was warmer than usual for that time of the year in Minnesota. It was a beautiful sunny day. A day when you could wear a sweatshirt outside and not feel cold. No snow had fallen yet, and people were still outside enjoying different activities.

I'm not a super-snuggly person when I sleep. Nor am I a morning person, for that matter. But for whatever reason, Andy moved over to my side of the bed that morning, and we snuggled for almost a half hour. I take this as a gift from God. We got to have that final moment together. A peaceful and quiet moment wrapped in each other's arms, just the two of us. Sometimes now when I'm sleeping alone in my bed, I lay just as we did that morning, pretending Andy is with me.

Andy let me sleep in as he got up to make pancakes, which was our usual Saturday tradition. We had a nice day planned. Later that afternoon, we planned to drive over to visit friends.

But first, Andy planned to head out to Lake Waconia to take pictures. This local lake was one of the things that had drawn us to our home. Anywhere you lived in the town of Waconia, it felt as if you lived on "the lake."

As Andy was getting ready for his day adventure, he popped in the bedroom. I was crying as I watched the last episode of *Gilmore Girls*. (I want to blame it on pregnancy hormones, but I'm sure I would have been crying regardless.) Not realizing why I was crying, Andy came over to the bed, very concerned. He asked if I was OK. We both laughed as I told him it was nothing but the show.

As he searched for a pair of long underwear, we talked about how long he would be out at the lake. He looked at me and said, "I should only be gone for two hours, don't you think?" We planned to head over to our friends' place at three.

Andy headed out of the room, only to realize a little while later that he needed to grab one last thing before he left. So he came dancing back into the room wearing a goofy smile and the Troll-doll hat Ike had gotten from a birthday party the weekend before. Of course, I burst into laughter.

That is the last memory I have of him alive. A grown man dancing in a Troll hat. God, I love that man. He said goodbye to the kids, as he always did, and told Ike that he would show him the pictures he took when he got home.

After I finished watching my show, I took a shower. The kids were playing in their rooms. Again, it was a normal Saturday in our house.

Just one day. One damn day that changed our lives completely and forever. One day that took away a lifetime of love and laughter in our home. It only takes one day, one moment, and everything you know, plan, and dream about is gone in an instant. Gone without you even being able to say goodbye.

As I finished showering, I spent time trying to find something to wear. I was in that in-between stage in my pregnancy—I wasn't really showing, but I was having a hard time buttoning my regular pants. I ended up wearing a brand-new top and sweater, which later I could never bear to wear again. I had to donate them.

Around noon, I started thinking it would be nice if we had time to stop for lunch on the way over to our friends' house. I called Andy. He didn't answer. At the time, I wasn't worried.

A half hour later, I tried calling again. Still no answer. Not worried yet. Though I was starting to get a little annoyed. If he didn't get home soon, we wouldn't be able to stop to eat.

As the time went on, the calls started going directly to voicemail. His phone wasn't even ringing. This was a little strange to me. It was very unlike him to not answer or for his phone to be dead. He always got so frustrated when I didn't have my phone.

Around one thirty, I started to get angry. I told myself that if he was not home by two, I would drive over to the lake and see what was taking him so long.

Two o'clock came and went.

Ike was sitting in the living room with me. He told me he had seen Daddy put the paddleboard on the car. I was a bit surprised by this. Andy hadn't mentioned paddleboarding when we spoke earlier.

I try not to beat myself up about this. I have no idea how I would have reacted if I had known he was going out on the paddleboard. It was *November*. But again, it was an unseasonably nice day. Would I have stopped him? I really don't know. It doesn't matter now. I try not to dwell on the what-ifs.

Time ticked on as we sat there waiting for Andy to return. "Where is your daddy?" I asked Ike.

I am sorry to even write this, but he replied, "He's probably dead."

"Why would you ever say that?" I snapped back.

To this day, I don't know why Ike made that comment or what it meant. We never talked about death, other than a great-grandma passing away.

Ike left the room to go play. It was about two forty-five. I told myself I would go to the lake if he was not back by three. Our original plan was to leave for our friends' place at three.

But now I was starting to get anxious. It was not like Andy to be gone for so long and to not answer the phone—especially when we had plans later in the day.

Three o'clock came. No Andy.

This will sound crazy, but my life is crazy, so I'm going to share it anyway: as I sat there in my living room, I had a vision. It was a terrifying vision of me arriving at the lake, seeing the car and the empty paddleboard, and screaming as I looked for him.

I threw on one of Andy's jackets and told Grace to watch her brother. I tried my best to be as calm as possible for my children. They didn't suspect anything was wrong.

I tried to push my thoughts out of my head, but I was shaking and crying as I drove to the lake. I pulled up and saw our car. The car we had bought together earlier in the year to prepare for our new baby boy.

I pulled past the car and the parking lot and drove onto the little gravel road adjacent to the lake. That's when my worst nightmare, my worst déjà vu moment, was realized. I saw it. The paddleboard floating on the lake.

Empty.

The rest of the story is a bit blurry. In some moments, it feels as if time were standing still. In other moments, it feels as if I were detached from reality. As if this could not be happening to me. As if I would wake up from this nightmare and have my family back.

I still have those moments when it seems this life can't *really* be mine. For a second, it feels like I'll somehow snap out of this, and there Andy will be, annoying me just as he used to. But that's not in the cards for me.

I do remember jumping out of my car and immediately going into fight mode. The adrenaline, stress, and anxiety going through my body was unlike anything I had ever felt. I started screaming from the top of my lungs, "ANDY! ANDY!

ANDY!" I didn't stop yelling his name as I ran. Writing these words doesn't do justice to the horror and panic in my voice.

This can't be happening, I thought. *I'm losing my mind. He's probably on the beach. Or if he did fall off the board, he's in the brush along the lake.*

I started running, looking up and down the side of the lake near where the paddleboard was located. I was screaming, shaking, and pleading as I ran. I had never been in a moment as intense as this, where I literally did not know what to do.

I pulled out my phone, ready to call 911. The rational side of me thought, *Andy will be so mad at me for calling 911 because this isn't really an emergency. I'm overreacting. He's here somewhere, just taking pictures.* But the pit I had in my stomach told me otherwise.

I quickly dialed 911. I told the operator that I had arrived at the lake to find the empty paddleboard but not my husband. I shared this story in between my panicking gasps and continuing to call out Andy's name.

I then called Ann, my neighbor and best friend. I quickly told her I could not find Andy. I asked her to get my children because they were still home alone.

After what felt like an eternity but also a sheer second, I could hear sirens approaching. The first officer, a young woman, arrived at the scene to find me screaming, crying, shaking, and begging for my husband. I pleaded for Andy, to see him somewhere, to know he was somewhere other than in that lake.

This was a moment I have not shared with many people. This was a moment I would not want anyone to witness. This was a moment of pure horror and devastation.

I don't know what I told the officer, but I do know I needed human contact. I felt so scared and alone. I asked the officer if I could hug her. It ended up being an awkward embrace. I could tell that this young officer had never been in a moment like this.

Other officers arrived. So did Ann. Ann's husband was now safely with my children. We immediately embraced. There were no words to exchange.

I continued to pace. Later, Ann shared with me that I kept saying, "I want to die. I want to die. I can't be alone." Being alone was now my greatest fear—and it would continue to be throughout my widowhood.

More officers, firefighters, and first responders began to arrive at the scene. I felt as if I were having an out-of-body experience. I could hear the sirens. I could see the officers formulating their search and rescue plans. But I just stood and watched, shaking, pleading to God, and still repeatedly calling out Andy's name as Ann tried to console me.

I knew I had to call family. I called my parents. I fell to my knees in the field next to the lake. I remember repeating "Daddy! Daddy! Daddy!" as I told him Andy was missing. I felt like a little child again, as if my mom and dad could take away this pain, just as they once were able to do years ago. But this pain was now my journey, my cross to bear. No one would ever be able to fix it.

My dad remarked months later that he knew something terrible had happened because I hadn't called him Daddy since I was a little girl.

As the first hour dragged on, it started to get cold and dark. They had now brought an ambulance onto the scene. The ambulance driver embraced me and Ann and asked if he could pray with us.

As I look back at this moment, I realize praying was the only thing we could do. I remember how much I appreciated that man and the power of that moment. It gave me a sliver of comfort. Just being there with the ambulance driver and Ann helped me see how there is such good in people. It helped me see how, even at that moment of unthinkable terror, God was with me. He was showing himself and giving me comfort through Ann and through this ambulance driver. He was with me. I was not alone. He never left my side.

As it got colder, I eventually ended up sitting in the ambulance, waiting for the news to come. My shouting for Andy had temporarily stopped.

Other family members started to arrive. There was a mixture of hugging, crying, and faces full of the worry and concern you never want to see on your loved ones. With swollen eyes and tissues soaked in tears, I laid my head on the shoulder of whoever was sitting next to me. In particular, I remember laying it on my mother's shoulder, feeling like a lost child. Feeling so empty, scared, and utterly alone.

Sheriffs and officers came in and out of the ambulance to share updates and search plans with me. It was like a movie playing in front of me. But it wasn't a movie. It was my life.

By this time, all my family and Andy's family had arrived. There was an event center by the lake that was often used to host weddings and other celebrations. Once the owner arrived, our group was quickly ushered inside.

I can imagine all the happy times and memories the place had held and still holds. But to me, it will forever be a holding cell, a place to which I never want to return, a place where I spent countless hours praying, sobbing, and screaming at God to please find my Andy.

Time stretched as the search continued. I remember officers telling me that if Andy had indeed drowned, they would find him quickly. The water was eerily calm—so still it looked like glass. As disgusting as this is to say, the conditions were perfect for finding a body—*my husband's* body. So the fact that they hadn't found him gave us such confidence and hope.

What also gave us hope was that they found his keys, camera, and phone on the bottom of the lake directly under the board. But no Andy. Again, we thought this was a good sign. If he had drowned, he would have been there with the keys, camera, and phone, right? But he wasn't. This had to mean he was somewhere on land. He *must* have made it to land.

But all that hope and confidence was followed by confusion as the night dragged on with no Andy. There were countless rescue teams, including some with dogs. They had boats and equipment searching both land and water. If he was in the water, they should have been able to find him.

Where was he?

It got later and later, yet still no Andy. Eventually, teams were sent home. It was getting colder, and officers were getting tired. We were told we should go home too and try to get some rest.

Rest! *Rest?* It was unfathomable to me.

My husband is out there somewhere! I thought. *It's cold. He could be dying right now. And I have to go home and rest? Why are we stopping? I should be looking!*

Eventually I was persuaded to go home. Searching would continue right away the next morning, they told me. Most importantly, I couldn't just think of me. I was seventeen weeks pregnant, so I had to try to rest my body.

But rest was the last thing that occurred in my home. My mom, dad, and mother-in-law stayed at my house with me. My children were still at Ann's house for a "sleepover," totally unaware of the situation.

I went to my room. But my body was pumping with so much adrenaline and anxiety that all I could do was pace and plead to God. Even my dog could not sit still. She could sense my anxiety. She paced with me.

I tried to lie in the bed Andy and I had snuggled in mere hours ago, but I couldn't do it. I couldn't be alone. So I went to the living room, where my mom and mother-in-law lay sleeping. This is where I would sleep for the next three weeks and four days.

By morning, I had to decide what to do with the kids—what to say to them. I couldn't think straight. I knew I couldn't just keep them at Ann's while we went back to the lake. Typically, the kids came right home the morning after a sleepover. They'd quickly figure out something was up. They would wonder where Daddy and Mommy were.

I decided I had to tell them the truth. I called Ann and had her send the kids home. I asked my parents and mother-in-law to allow me to speak to them alone first.

I paced, waiting on pins and needles for what seemed like an eternity for them to come walking through the door. I began to talk to Andy and God. I remember saying in such a gentle whisper, "I have to tell the babies now, Andy. I have to tell the babies." I pleaded to God to give me guidance, for I was about to crush their innocent little bubble on life.

I greeted them at the entry. They were bubbly and smiley—they had no clue what had transpired within not even twenty-four hours. I asked them to sit with me on the floor in the entry. I didn't have the energy to make it to the couch. And if I didn't say it right then, would I ever be able to?

I looked in their big beautiful eyes and said, "Daddy is missing." I wanted to be hopeful—but honest. So I added, "Daddy is most likely in the water."

There were immediate cries of pain from their sweet little lips. All I can remember them saying is, "I don't want to be a one-parent family."

How could I disagree?

The only thing I could do was hold them. That's a mom's

job. But I couldn't take away their pain, just as my mom and dad couldn't take away mine.

This was the first but not the last time I had to tell them their daddy was dead.

(Really, God?)

Chapter 6

THREE WEEKS AND FOUR DAYS

Andy was missing three weeks and four days. I can't fathom how I ever survived that time. Emotions were so heightened and anxieties were so high. You wouldn't think a body could sustain it—let alone a pregnant body. Somehow, I did it.

I often tell myself that if I could make it through those three weeks, then I could do just about anything. There is some sense of consolation that I should never have such a dark period of time like that again (I hope).

Those three weeks and four days began with searching, searching, and more searching: drones, dogs, boats, divers, sonar, helicopters, men and women combing miles of land. The event center served as a makeshift command center. It was abuzz with activity.

I took my shift daily. Many times, I would have a flash of realization: *Wait—they are looking for* my *husband.* It was all too much to wrap my mind around.

As Andy's family and friends, we all wanted to be out searching too. But this was not allowed until the professionals had done a thorough investigation and sweep of the area. The last thing we needed was for one of us to throw off any clues or get hurt while trying to find Andy. So all we could do was wait. And wait was exactly what we did.

The first night Andy was missing, I took respite in the front entrance of the event center, which was separate from the ballroom. As the hours and days and weeks went on, this spot continued to give me some comfort. When being around others felt overwhelming, I could escape there to be alone, to cry, to yell, to sit in silence, and to pray. Others seemed to sense this was my spot and allowed it to be just mine.

This was where Jim, the sheriff, would give me updates. I became very close to Jim. He is one of the kindest men you will ever meet. He and Detective Chris were my go-to guys. Every day, they kept me informed about procedures and the searching process as well as any leads or updates.

Jim and I developed a code for when he needed to update me or ask questions. We needed this code because every time the door opened and someone from the search crew came in, I'd flood with anxiety and hope. My eyes and heart would whisper, *Did you find him?* In those early days, I had such hope we would find Andy alive. But every time, the other person's eyes would give me the same answer—*no*—and my waiting would continue.

So whenever Sheriff Jim entered my respite place to speak to me, he'd immediately shake his head, wave his hands, and repeat "No, nothing." Seeing this sign would instantly calm me. But it was still a code, a language, I never wanted to learn or need.

Sheriff Jim gave me as much comfort as one could feel while their spouse was missing. But it wasn't just Jim. It was also Chris and the countless firefighters, police officers, volunteers, search and rescue teams, paramedics, and others. They poured their hearts and souls into searching for Andy. They handled this missing person case with such care, compassion, and love. It felt as if they too knew Andy and he was a part of their own family.

There's so much negativity in the press regarding police officers. Why aren't these men and women celebrated? As I've said before, people are good. I wasn't alone, even if I felt that way. God was with me, and he was showing himself in these men and women who spent countless hours trying to help me and my family.

Throughout these first days of waiting, I'd occasionally feel a surge of energy, almost a *need* to do something, to be out looking for Andy myself. I'm not sure what would prompt me, but several times I would burst out of my special spot in the front entrance and run outside. Oftentimes, someone would be trailing right behind me.

Once outside, I would scream Andy's name. If he could just hear *my* voice—the voice of his college sweetheart, the voice of his children's mother, the voice of the person he loved more than anyone else—maybe I could bring him back. Maybe he would somehow gather enough strength and energy to call out.

There were also times when I would race out, curse God's name, and use more profanity than you'd ever want your mother to hear. It was a release—even if only a little—of the pent-up sadness, anger, despair, and hopelessness bursting at the seams and needing to escape my weak body.

Nothing would come from these outbursts but tears and a return to my safe zone. Someone would gather me in their arms—my dad, brother, mom, friend, or relative—and bring me back to the dreaded event center.

I also found myself listening to two songs over and over. One was our wedding song: "The Luckiest" by Ben Folds. If I played it enough, perhaps Andy would hear it. He'd walk through the door, we'd immediately embrace, and he'd sing the lyrics to me, as he had done so many times before while we danced in our bedroom.

The other song, "Be Not Afraid," was a hymn I had heard countless times in church growing up. It brought me comfort when I was in such a state of fear. It was almost as if this song had been written for me. God knew one of his children was intensely hurting, so he sent this song to help remind me that he was still there helping me, holding me, and protecting Andy.

> *If you pass through raging waters in the sea, you shall not drown.*
>
> *If you walk amid the burning flames, you shall not be harmed.*

If you stand before the pow'r of hell and death is at your side,

know that I am with you through it all.

The first few days came and went with no leads. Each day led to a night without answers nor sleep. I would head home with such a sense of helplessness. Each night, I knew Andy could be out there—literally freezing to death, fighting for his life, waiting for me to find him—and all I was doing was lying on a mattress on my living room floor.

Just as time marched on, so did the seasons. November was giving way to December. It may have been unseasonably warm the day Andy disappeared, but now the weather was changing. The cold was creeping in—and with it an impending sense of doom. The water would freeze, and the searching would stop. This stomach-wrenching fear gripped me each night.

Each morning, searching continued. Other aspects of this missing person case needed to be addressed as well, though. Missing person flyers were printed and displayed at every business in Waconia and in many of the surrounding towns. Imagine bringing your child to dinner or the grocery store, where they see a missing person flyer with their daddy on it.

Other avenues of the investigation were pursued too. Questions needed to be asked—questions you never want to answer. Was this staged? Did Andy run off? Was it a suicide?

These parts of the investigation were the most challenging to swallow, but they had to be ruled out.

Andy's computer and bank account were looked at, airports were contacted, and all leads big and small were investigated. I had to search for Andy's passport and rummage through his office desk to look for any clues.

Every time we found items or information that disproved any of these theories, it brought huge sighs of relief and reassurance. There was no way Andy could have ever *done this* to the precious people he lived and breathed for.

But still, as I sat in my safe zone at the event center night and day, my mind would take me to places. My mind would fill with thoughts and theories and doubts. I'd try to bury or push them out as soon as they entered, but they still came. They came with a vengeance that brought me to my knees, knocked all my breath away, and left me a pile on the floor, unable to be collected. And the longer Andy was missing, the more these thoughts came and left insanity in their wake.

By day four or five, the sheriff's department decided to discontinue the large, sweeping ground search. They felt the surrounding land had been thoroughly searched, with no results. Rather, they would now focus the search primarily on the lake, as that was the number-one place the police expected Andy would be found.

And so dogs, drones, sonar, boats, divers, volunteer specialty services from Bruce's Legacy, fishing guides, and the dive crew from Saint Louis County all continued searching. No one had given up hope that Andy would be found. The best of the best was out searching the water. But there were still no leads, no evidence, nothing.

While the officials focused their search on the lake, I held on to the glimmer of hope that Andy had not drowned, that he was instead alive somewhere out there on land, waiting for us to find him. It was urgent, then, that the ground search continue, even if it meant doing it on our own.

I called a family meeting. I sat and looked at the faces of our most loved people. We all looked so desperate, tired, and baffled. We needed a plan. I don't remember much from that conversation. All I can recall saying was that I wanted the ground search to continue.

It was my call to make, after all. At the end of the day, our friends and family could go back to their normal lives, go back to work, and continue their daily routines. Yes, they would feel a void—the loss of a son, brother, friend. But my life had forever changed. All my daily routines, my normal life, were impacted in every single aspect. It was *my* husband who was missing and who was my whole life.

So we were allowed to conduct a search of our own. We enlisted all our able-bodied friends, family, and coworkers. We were advised to limit the number of people for safety reasons. If they had allowed more people, we would have had the entire town searching.

It felt like an episode of *CSI* as my sister-in-law plotted and planned where a search crew would walk on foot. I remember being in a trauma-induced state as I listened from the back of the crowd. This crew was plotting to search for a missing person—*my* person. It was as if I hadn't realized this was all about Andy until that very moment.

As hopeful as I was about finding Andy, I was also filled with such dread and panic as we began the search. It felt like a race for his life. If Andy had somehow managed to crawl into a marsh or the woods, he would have been lying out there without food, water, and shelter for over four days. If we couldn't find him that day, I feared he would surely die alone.

I fought intensely with Sheriff Jim and my dad about going out in the woods to join the search myself. Both of them were adamant. They did not want me—at seventeen weeks pregnant—to go. But my heart was screaming that I *had* to go. If Andy were out there, he would hear my voice calling him.

I did go out one time. Much to my dismay, though, I eventually agreed it wasn't a wise idea for me to be trudging around in the rough terrain. I also knew that Andy would be so angry with me. He never would have allowed me to be out there.

So I once again took respite in my "resting" place in the front entrance of the event center. I waited on pins and needles for any bit of news from the search crews.

It was a time of intense emotions, anxieties, fears—and also laughter. Yes, laughter. It helped us cope. My brother and I lovingly named my mother "crazy lake lady" for her antics during the search. My mom was obviously devastated and emotional, and she would often get lost as she frantically searched out in the woods. This caused much turmoil for the rest of us, because she had to be picked up by the search crew in their ATV. But it also caused belly laughter when they'd find her praying by a tree, wearing a stocking hat with her hair in her eyes.

We also had some laughs about the psychic. (You read that right: I said *psychic*. When your husband is missing, you will try just about anything.) She had us convinced that Andy was hiding out somewhere in a bunker, wearing green war paint. So my mother-in-law, my mom, and I took off with the psychic to investigate this vision.

Can you imagine three adult women and one psychic driving through Waconia searching for a bunker? In my head, I knew it was crazy, and we all ended up laughing when we got home. I joked to my mother-in-law that if Andy truly had escaped to a bunker just to get away from me, there'd be hell to pay when he decided to emerge from said bunker. She may not have found this funny, but I did.

But then the sun began setting, and each of the crews returned empty-handed and empty-hearted. I felt so hopeless. There was nothing I could do. Nothing.

In a blur, days turned to weeks. Searching did not stop, but options were limited now that the lake had frozen. The sheriff called each day to update me on the daily plans and leads—if any. Each time his name appeared on my phone, my heart would sink to my stomach.

Countless news stations contacted me to share my story. I agreed to be interviewed, even though I didn't know how it would go. But I wanted to share Andy's story so searching would continue.

The interviews were gut-wrenching, but I was able to keep my composure. That was something I was learning to do. I had to master my composure; otherwise, I would have been crying all the time.

Wherever I went, so many people knew who I was and knew my story. I was in so many people's hearts and prayers. Mind you, I will never say *anything* negative about all the love and support I received. But it was a challenge to be constantly hugged, to have people cry when talking to me, and to constantly answer the "How are you?" questions. I began to feel severe anxiety whenever I left the house. As much as I knew people were well-meaning, I just wanted to disappear. That was so unlike me.

My friends and family were such a huge support system. You really know who your friends are when tragedy occurs. My kids were cared for. My fridge was always full. Christmas lights were hung. Maternity clothes were delivered.

My very best childhood friend even flew in from out of state just to join the search. She stayed throughout the whole process, giving up time away from work and her family. Many of my other friends would just show up to do tasks I did not even realize needed to be done nor did I have the energy to complete.

They supported me any way they could. Their efforts were tireless, especially because I knew their hearts were hurting as well. Their friendship, kindness, time, monetary gifts, compassion, and love are things I can never repay. I feel so blessed to call these people—*my people*—friends.

Every week that passed without finding Andy was another week of my pregnancy progressing. I was roughly halfway through my pregnancy, which is a very critical time. I joked a lot that God planned for me to be pregnant when Andy disappeared, otherwise I would have become an alcoholic. (OK, this probably isn't a good joke. I totally understand why alcohol is a very big problem for widows and widowers.)

Because my body was under complete stress, I went to the doctor just to make sure my baby was surviving all this trauma. I had a new doctor for this third pregnancy. We had met only a few times at earlier pregnancy checkups.

My two childhood friends accompanied me to the appointment. We joked all the way there about how they would end up as my labor coaches as well.

But once I walked into the doctor's office, all the composure I had been working so hard to keep quickly disintegrated into a puddle of tears. Even though he hardly knew me, my doctor entered the room with such compassion in his eyes. We hugged for a long time as I cried as if I had been holding it in for a lifetime. I am forever grateful for this doctor and his wife, who became my pediatrician.

This is yet another example of the support that helped me get through these moments. Family, friends, doctors, sheriffs, and strangers carried me when I felt as if I couldn't walk on my own. If you ever needed proof of God's existence, these people are a prime example. They truly bore the face of Jesus with their love and compassion.

In particular, I would not have survived without my immediate family and in-laws. Like every family, we have our struggles, disagreements, and differences. But man, when shit hit the fan, when the going got tough, when life threw me the biggest curveball ever, *they were there*. It's as simple as that. Whatever my children and I needed, I could count on them.

That's what family is for and should be. I know not everyone has this kind of support, though. That's why I will be forever grateful for the love, help, and support they gave and continue to give me and my children. I owe so much gratitude to my family and am forever indebted to them for their love and continued support. From the moment Andy went missing, they helped me tread this complicated path. When called upon—and often even without being called upon—they were there. I could always, and I mean *always*, count on their unconditional love.

My brothers and their families took my children in as their own during the searching and anytime I just could not mother them as they needed. My brothers took time away from their work and family to help their baby sister in any way possible. Andy's mom moved to Waconia just to love and support me. Andy's brothers and dad provided constant male role-modeling for my children, attending their sporting events, wrestling them, and overall just reminding them of who their daddy was.

I do believe family means more than just genetics or relation through marriage. I consider my neighbor Ann a sister. She has played such an intimate part in my story and continues to do so to this day. Ann was my very first good friend when I moved to Waconia. Her family is my family. Her husband cared for my children while we were up at the lake during the search. Her children and my children treat each other as siblings. A day doesn't seem to go by without one of our children plopping down on the other's couch or digging through a snack cupboard.

Ann was the first person to arrive on the scene on that very terrible day. She picked me up off the ground and surrounded me with love and compassion. And just as she was with me on one of the worst days of my life, she was with me on one of the best days of my life. She was in the delivery room for the birth of my baby. (More on that later.) She continues to support me through all life's ups and downs. And boy, do we love to laugh together!

I need to take a moment to specifically talk about the love of a parent. I always knew my parents loved me. But the love they have showed me through this experience is a *forever* love. They have shown such willingness to take care of me, even when I am a grown woman with a family of my own.

Watching their baby girl go through so much pain must have caused them such pain in return—especially because they were not able to take that pain away. It's a primal need to care for your offspring. Not being able to take away this deep, deep pain was such a heart-wrenching process for them.

I know this because as I was grieving, I was also mothering two young children. I could not take away their pain any more than my parents could take away mine. Watching those little people in so much pain and knowing there was nothing I could do—it killed me to my core. Like a literal knife to my heart.

Once you bring a beautiful child into this world, there is nothing you wouldn't do for them. That doesn't change as you get older. So to my mom and my dad: I know the pain you feel because I feel it too. It is horrible and gut-wrenching. Actually, there are no words to describe this deep ache you feel for your child.

What I have learned is that you can't take away the pain, but you can help ease it. Mom and Dad, you have eased this pain with your unconditional love. You were willing to drop anything for me and your grandchildren, to retire early so you could help me, to let me yell at you and cry on your shoulder, to simply be there for me so I could get through this dark time in my life. I know you will always be there. *No matter what.*

I can't express how grateful I am to have parents as loving as you. You have taught me how to love. But most importantly, you have taught me the love of our Father. Only through him—and him alone—can we survive such a tragedy as I have experienced. I thank you for that.

Family. Friends. Strangers. So many people surrounded me during those horrible days and weeks.

But still, there was no Andy.

Chapter 7

THE FISHERMAN AND THE FISHER OF MEN

He reached down from on high and seized me,
drew me out of the deep waters.

—2 Samuel 22:17

Despite all the searching for three weeks and four days, we still did not have Andy's body. The sheriff's department made plans for a crew to ice dive once the lake was solid enough for machinery to travel on it. This would not happen until after the holidays, which were days away. If ice diving did not produce any results, then we would have to wait until the spring to begin searching again.

At this point, my hope of Andy being found alive had dwindled. As much as I hated admitting it, I now knew the only place he could be was in the water. All the other options seemed so crazy and impossible. He would never run from us. He was not in a bunker. And who would kidnap a grown man, especially a bald one who grew his own loofahs?

I just wanted this nightmare to end. Not finding Andy left us in limbo. I couldn't move forward with a funeral.

God and I were certainly fighting at this point. It was hard enough to understand why my husband was most likely dead. But why did I also have to endure these treacherous weeks of searching, of the unknown? It was more than any human could handle. All I wanted was some tiny sliver of peace that the searching chapter of my life would be over. Then I could at least move forward to face my next nightmare: life without Andy.

My eldest brother, Chris, was a rock for me throughout those weeks. As always, he took care of his baby sister. He has a quiet but strong and ever so compassionate demeanor. We don't always need to talk; he just has a presence. When you are with him, things will be OK.

He's also a very smart man who works in the world of finance. He took charge of all the financial tasks I needed to accomplish. He set appointments with financial advisors and lawyers and attended each one to help me. He sat with me and worked out my finances, assuring me I would be able to take care of my little family. As a fiscally responsible man, Andy had purchased life insurance.

The funny thing about life insurance, though: you need a *body* to receive it.

The morning three weeks and four days after Andy's disappearance, I sat in my car on a gravel road, sobbing. I was on the phone with Chris, and we had just talked to the individuals handling Andy's life insurance. We suddenly realized that without finding Andy, it could take *years* to receive any of the life insurance owed to me.

My mind went to all the worst imaginable places: losing my house, having to move out of my beloved neighborhood, uprooting the children, not being able to support my new baby, a life so unthinkable. I had thought my reality couldn't get worse. But this newest reality was devastating.

"It's too hard, Lord," I said out loud. "Please take me too."

Of course, I felt jaded thinking such a thing. I couldn't make that choice even if I wanted to. I had these little people to take care of. I was stuck in this life with no way out.

As I had done each day before, I gathered myself and drove home. I had people who relied on me. I would have to figure out how to take care of them. Grabbing the tissues in my car, which had now become a necessity, I wiped my endless tears and went home.

I think that was when God stepped in. Not that he hadn't been there the whole time, mind you. But at that moment, I think he said, "Enough is enough." Little did I know what would happen that evening.

As the day progressed, I went in for my first ultrasound. Originally, the appointment had been scheduled for the week before, but I had to cancel. As if I didn't have enough on my plate at the time, I also came down with a bad case of the stomach flu. (This seems like another good place for a "Really, God?")

Andy and I had always planned to take the kids to our first ultrasound appointment, to make a great family experience of all of us seeing our new little boy. I did still take the kids and also my mom. It was such a special moment—but a moment I so desperately wanted to share with my husband. There was an unending ache in my heart, a feeling of something missing.

I'd feel that way for every special moment I would now encounter. Each holiday and birthday. All the firsts for my children. Each special event would carry that bittersweet sensation. This is what so many don't understand about grief and why it can never be on a timeline. Even years later, the wounds from missing a loved one can feel so fresh.

After the appointment, we headed home, Mom included. (She really was a constant at the house.) The kids went off to play, and I started sending ultrasound pictures to family and friends.

Then the sheriff texted me: "Can I stop over?" My heart sank into my stomach. Jim and I typically had conversations over the phone, not at the house.

I called Ann and asked if she could pick up my kids, explaining that the sheriff was coming over with news. She was at a friend's house, but she left her kids there and flew in her car to my aid. My kids would feel so safe with her. I needed them to be with her.

Jim arrived within ten minutes. Mom was with me when he delivered the news.

My Andy was finally found.

I can't for the life of me remember whether I cried or what I said in that moment. It was strange to feel gut-wrenching sadness and relief at the same time.

The heaviest weight I had been carrying was finally relieved, though instantly replaced with a new weight I would forever carry: the weight of widowhood. One of the heaviest weights possible for a human to carry. A label that would forever define me. A new box I had to check on all paperwork. A story I would have to tell when asked about my husband or my marital status. A conversation I would have to have with all my children's teachers. An empty bed I would have to sleep alone in every night. It was a weight no thirty-five-year-old woman should have to carry. The weight of utter loneliness.

Jim sat down and explained that Travis, a fisherman, had gone out on the lake that evening to do some ice fishing. He drilled his hole, then lowered his underwater ice-fishing camera into the water. As he looked at the camera's monitor, he didn't see fish; he saw Andy's boots.

Retrieval efforts would begin immediately. But until they had the body, Jim could not 100 percent confirm it was Andy. But, he joked, if there were other bodies in Lake Waconia, then the sheriff's department hadn't been doing their job. (He knew his audience.)

Travis had previously helped with the search, actually. He had shared tips about spots where Andy could be and the layout of the lake. He was a fishing guide by trade and a man of God. I was told he had been praying for my family throughout those weeks of searching.

I really do believe our Lord—the true Fisher of Men— sent Fisherman Travis to find my Andy, when countless volunteers and experts who found missing people for a living could not. Lake Waconia is huge—the second largest in the Twin Cities metro area. That Travis drilled a hole at the right spot and saw Andy's feet on his camera was nothing but divine intervention.

On the day that began with me sobbing in my car on a gravel road, wanting to die, God sent Travis fishing to find Andy. I will be forever thankful to Travis. He eased our pain and gave us peace, knowing the search was finally over.

On November 26, 2016, Jesus reached into the waters, pulled my husband close to him, and brought him to the most unimaginably glorious place. And on December 20, 2016, I finally found peace in *knowing* he was with Jesus.

Ironically, the idea of Jesus reaching into the water was not new to me. A year earlier, I had selected a phone screensaver depicting Jesus with his arm extended underwater. As someone who struggled with anxiety, I liked the idea of Jesus taking hold of my hand whenever I felt "underwater."

Little did I know this image would be so much more impactful.

The screensaver was just further proof that Jesus had indeed reached into the waters and pulled Andy to heaven. One day, I will join Andy in that glorious place. From deep within my soul, pushing through my numbness, comes a smile that yearns for that day.

But God tells me I have so much more to do on this earth—and I will do it! God has plans for me. More glorious than I can ever imagine. I will keep believing this and trusting in God. I know he is always there with me. With him, I will never fall. I will have a future. No, it won't be the future I had planned with Andy. But I have faith in the future the Lord is giving me.

But on that night we found Andy, there was no time to think about the future. I had to make the dreaded phone calls to family and close friends. It seemed all too unfair. I had to tell them—again—that Andy had died.

I could hear both pain and relief in the voice of each family member and friend. We all knew Andy was in the lake, but we had held on to hope that our husband, father, son, brother, and friend was still somehow alive. My call confirmed that the hope was now gone, but at least the pain of the unknown was gone as well.

Ann still recalls the road she was driving on and the moment when I whispered the news: "They found Andy in the lake." After all of this, how could this woman and I not be bonded for life? She is now my family.

I did not cry as I made these calls. I had already learned the skill of reining in my emotions. Or maybe it was just the utter loss of feeling. Until Andy's death, I had no clue what numbness felt like. I have unfortunately now mastered this feeling. Some days I am so numb that I can't even cry. I think I had one of those moments as I made the calls. I floated above this body as "she" called all her most important people.

Immediate family members came to my house as we yet again waited for Andy to come home. This time, we knew he would. There was peace in that.

Retrieving a body from a frozen lake does not happen quickly. Jim sat with us the entire time as we waited for the news that Andy was out of the lake.

Jim had spent countless hours trying to find Andy—going so above and beyond his call of duty. For weeks, he had listened to every crazy whim or lead I came across. And now he sat like a part of the family as our Andy was pulled out of the lake. Jim was a calming force in an insane storm of emotions. This job is his calling, and I believe Jesus placed him in this position to help me and others through the most terrible moments of our lives. He is a great man, and I will be forever grateful for his kindness, compassion, and determination to never give up until Andy was found.

As the hours started to pass and close family started to arrive, I knew this would be a long process into the night. I had to talk to my babies. I had to tell them—for the second time—that their daddy, their comforter, their wrestling partner, was dead. Not "likely" dead, as I had indicated the first time. This time, he was *dead*.

I drove over to Ann's, with my mother along.

I'm not exactly sure how I phrased it to them. It's all such a blinding blur in my mind. A conversation I, as a parent, never knew I'd have to have with my children, let alone twice.

For Ike, there was shouting and many, many tears. But Grace pretended the news didn't bother her. Instead, she acted excited to sleep at her cousin's house.

A mother knows her children better than anyone in the world. I knew she always held her emotions. I finally had to stop her.

"This is enough," I said. "You need to stop pretending this isn't bothering you."

Immediately, she started sobbing in my arms. I felt both the release and relief in her cries. At that moment, she needed only what her mother could provide—love and comfort.

I know in my heart Andy's death was a terrible accident. One thing I do not know, however, is why I must carry the weight of *two* death anniversaries, why I had to tell my children *twice* that their daddy was dead. It's unfair. I don't understand.

I guess faith isn't about having all the answers. Rather, it's simply about trusting that God is in charge and taking care of us. I try to remember this true meaning of faith whenever I wallow in the challenging days of grief. Yet the pain is still there, and the questions are hard to swallow.

The night proceeded on as we waited for the news. You could see such a mixture of relief and sadness in each loved one's face. We sat and talked. There was laughter. My mom and mother-in-law each had a much-needed beer. I was so filled with adrenaline that I occasionally had to go upstairs to get away from the chatter.

Throughout this process, I was warned that Andy's body would most likely not be in its normal state when he was pulled out of the water. Andy had been submerged in ice-cold water for over three weeks. And once he was removed, no one knew how quickly he would begin to deteriorate. I was advised to not see him until he was at the funeral home.

After hours and hours, he was finally out of the water. The coroner arrived on the scene at the lake. She called Jim and said she needed some way to identify the body, as Andy didn't have any identifying information on him.

We were worried they'd need to examine dental records, which would drag out the process. But then my dad came up with the brilliant idea to identify him by his tattoos on his back.

Then the coroner came to the house, as she had to ask me some questions. We sat at my kitchen table—the same table where Andy and my children had enjoyed countless loving meals filled with laughter.

After her questions came to an end, I asked one of my own: "How did he look?"

"I've never seen a picture of Andy," she said, "but I'd say he looked pretty good."

The hair on my body immediately stood up. I had an intense reaction in my soul.

I needed to see him.

I needed to see him *now*.

I yelled. I screamed. I forcefully demanded they take me to him—before God only knew what would happen to his body.

Later, my mom told me how proud she was of me in that moment. She said she didn't know whether she would have or could have been so strong and forceful in the same situation.

But no matter how proud she was of me, no matter how much I demanded, I was not allowed to see my husband that night. It was not possible, they informed me. There was some rule about not opening the body bag once it was zipped. Instead, I was guaranteed that I could view him at the medical examiner's office first thing in the morning.

After three weeks and four days, Andy had finally been found. All those glimmers of hope were now dead, like him. His body was the only thing I had left. But now someone else was in charge of the man to whom I had given my life in our wedding vows. It was as if he were never mine. How could someone keep me from seeing him?

We hadn't done anything wrong.

I guess you could say I tried to sleep that night. But again, I had so much adrenaline pumping through my body that I probably could have lifted a car. The next morning slowly approached. I could not get in the car quickly enough.

My mom and mother-in-law came with me. When we pulled into the parking lot, a very strange feeling came over me. I would finally be in a building where Andy was. After so much searching, wondering, and worrying, we would finally be together.

Of course, this was not how I had envisioned it would go. But I did experience a sense of peace knowing I would finally see him. At one point, I didn't think I would ever see his face again.

We sat in the waiting room as they completed the preparation for our viewing. The medical examiner then escorted us to another waiting room outside the room where Andy lay. I would go in first. My mother-in-law wasn't sure if she could see him if he didn't look like "Andy."

But nothing would stop me from seeing my husband.

I entered the room to a body covered with a white sheet lying on a metal table. The medical examiner had tucked the sheet down to under his armpits.

I remember the distinct smell in the air. It was a smell of death—both sweet and pungent. Andy was still frozen, preserved so much that the decomposition obviously hadn't begun. But the smell was still was strong enough to linger in my nose after leaving. This was not the smell of a man who commonly took two showers a day.

The medical examiner shut the door and let me have my moment alone with Andy. My hands were trembling as I approached the love of my life.

"Here you are," I whispered out loud. "Finally, here you are."

Surprisingly, I didn't cry as I looked at him. He looked just as he always did, almost as if he were sleeping. He had his normal coloring, and even his lips were still pink and soft.

But then I touched his chest and felt his cold, hard body. This was not the same warm, soft man who had cradled me in his arms mere weeks ago as I cried about *Gilmore Girls*.

I stroked his cleanly trimmed beard and put my face near his. The whiskers that had once teasingly rubbed against my face still did the same. In fact, it was the one thing that remained the same from the time I viewed him at the medical examiner's office to the time his casket was closed at the funeral. The feeling of his whiskers became a comfort to me throughout the process of saying goodbye.

As he lay there on this cold metal bed, I inspected the rest of his body. His hands and feet were completely wrinkled and set with the beginnings of the rigor mortis process. His hands would later haunt me. I still experience flashbacks whenever I see hands that have spent too much time in the water.

Never in my wildest dreams did I ever think I would be caressing a dead body without thinking twice. But it was my husband lying there. I didn't want to leave him. I crouched over, leaning close, and quietly sang some of the lyrics from our wedding song into his ear: *"I am, I am, I am the luckiest."* I just wanted to stay and look at him, touch his arms, stroke his beard, feel his soft pink lips.

Before I left the room, I gave him a final kiss on the lips and whispered how much I loved him.

My mother-in-law and mom then took their turn viewing Andy's body. The entire time, I sat in disbelief that this was actually happening to me.

The medical examiner then gave me my last piece of Andy. A piece of Andy that I had given to him on one of the happiest days of our lives. His wedding band. I gripped this ring for dear life. It was the last thing Andy had been wearing, the last connection I had to him.

As we drove home, there was such a strange, thick feeling in the air. You could almost taste it. Finally, I could breathe. Oh, and eat. I mean, who *doesn't* stop at McDonald's for hash browns after they view their late husband's body?

That feeling in the air—it was relief.

Chapter 8

FUNERAL PLANNING: MY NEW SIDE GIG

Driving home from the medical examiner's office, we realized we needed to start making funeral arrangements. First of all, we needed to choose the funeral home that would receive Andy's body for its final preparations before burial.

As we approached Waconia, we drove by the lake and Paradise Lane. That's the road that leads to the beach access. The road I took that very first day, when I saw Andy's paddleboard floating there in the lake. The road I drove back and forth, back and forth, all those weeks of searching.

And here that road was now, as I was contemplating funeral arrangements on my way back from seeing my husband's body in the morgue. I could think of a million names for that road, but Paradise Lane was certainly not one of them.

I mean, come on—the name of the road is *Paradise Lane*! I suppose I should take that as a divine sign that Andy is in paradise. But nope. I think this deserves a "Really, God?"

When we returned home, I was greeted by sweet friends who had shown up without needing to be asked. It was nice having their comfort and support.

But moments later, the doorbell rang. It was the news station. Word was out that Andy had been found. The reporter asked if I could do an interview now.

By that time, I had already been on the news several times. I knew the routine: where they'd set up the microphone, the camera, the lighting. I knew how to keep my composure when on camera. But I literally had not showered or changed my clothes in days.

"I look horrible!" I confessed.

"It doesn't matter," he replied with a shrug.

I refused to go on TV looking like a crazy unkempt widow. I may have a dead husband, but I still have standards. (Yes, you can laugh at that. It's that sick widow humor.) The reporter said they would come back in a few hours, which gave me time to shower and get ready.

The interview went as well as an interview can go when you're talking about finding your husband's body. I'm not sure if I cried. Even to this day, I joke, "I don't cry anymore"—almost as if I cried enough in those weeks to last me a lifetime. Most likely, I was in shock throughout the whole interview and was using the "composure" skill I had now fine-tuned.

After the interview, we headed to the funeral home, where I began making decisions left and right. I'm sure Andy would have been dying (no pun intended) the entire time. Usually, I couldn't make a decision for the life of me.

For instance, every time Andy had to pick up dinner on the way home from work, I'd make him list off every option possible. Then I'd say no to each and every one. Finally, I'd tell him just to pick, but then I'd say no to that. Just one of those cute things I did that drove him crazy. Yet there at the funeral home, I was making decisions like nobody's business.

Looking back at those days, I have no idea how I made so many decisions and completed so many tasks in only a few short days. I can't take all the credit, of course. The people at the funeral home and my friends and family made the process easier. Still, there were things no one could do but me. I was the widow. I approached it as if it were a job.

I especially don't know how I accomplished it all right at Christmas. We began preparations on December 21. We scheduled the wake for December 26 and the funeral for December 27. Yep. Fa-la-la-la-la. Nothing captures the holiday spirit like a funeral.

But that was just the way it had to be. It had to happen as soon as possible, because we were racing against the decomposition clock and I desperately wanted an open casket. So many people needed the closure. They needed to actually see Andy after such a long search. But I mostly wanted my kids to see their dad one last time. Being able to see a loved one and say goodbye is so necessary in the grieving process, especially for children.

Once the funeral date was set, picking Andy's outfit was my next task. I loved what I chose for him. It was a light-gray slender-fit suit he had worn one week earlier on a work trip to Nashville.

However, the suit was stained. Andy had spilled beer on it when he went out with his coworkers. My friend volunteered to get the suit dry-cleaned. It was hard, though, letting go of that suit. I knew that the next time I would see it, he'd be wearing it in his casket. Oh, speaking of caskets—I was able to choose that without even batting an eye.

Next, we headed to meet a woman from my church who would help us pick out his cemetery plot. They asked me if I wanted to buy a plot next to his. Cue the gut punch. Nothing makes you evaluate your mortality like buying your own burial plot. I later joked with my sister-in-law that when I go on Match.com, I'll list that I come with my own plot. That should really reel the men in.

When it came time to design our joint stone, though, I couldn't bring myself to put my name on it with that open-ended "1981–" date. That just isn't something a thirty-five-year-old pregnant woman should have to ever do. So my side remains blank.

Some people have asked me, "What if you remarry? Will you still want to be buried next to Andy?" My answer is always yes. I want my children to be able to visit their parents together.

My next husband will just have to deal. After all, he'll be marrying me for my sexy burial plot anyway. Who knows— maybe he could be buried on top of me. We could end up in some weird burial plot threesome. It's really up in the air at this point.

My next step was to meet with the priest and plan the service. As I entered the priest's office, I had one thing on my mind: Dave Matthews Band.

Typically, Catholic services cannot include secular music. But Dave Matthews Band was Andy's all-time favorite. I wanted his casket carried out to "Ants Marching." It was the only funeral detail I even cared about. I had this picture in my head of Andy playing air guitar with all the angels joining in above us.

I was doing this for Andy. He needed it. *I* needed it. I gave my mom a pep talk, telling her she *would* be on my side. She was a little uneasy about it, but she agreed.

I was ready to fight tooth and nail for this. But luckily, we belong to a wonderful parish with a priest who had been with me throughout the journey. He allowed this young widow's request. I felt a sense of accomplishment. Andy would have been so proud of me for fighting for him.

But here's a little secret: I never really liked Dave Matthews that much before Andy died. But now the band is near and dear to my heart. I feel close to Andy whenever I hear them. In particular, I jam out to "Ants Marching" like no other song.

So Andy's getting the last laugh. He had to die before I liked Dave Matthews Band. What a sick twist.

The whirlwind of planning and preparations continued. As I said, I can't take all the credit. Our family and friends and everyone in the community were so wonderful during this time.

This included my school district, coworkers, students, and their families. I'm so lucky to be employed by and to work alongside such wonderful people. Andy's employer agreed to cater the meal, letting me choose whatever options I wanted. One of the local limo services gave us a limo for the procession from the church to the burial site. Some of the local veterans and Andy's Seventy-Ninth Military Police Company volunteered their time to participate in the services as well. Friends helped me with the slideshow, made meals for the family at the wake—I could go on and on.

As amazing as the outpouring was, I was still struggling anytime I went out of the house. No matter how caring people were, being in public made me anxious. I didn't want anyone to look at me or pity me. I could see it in their eyes. It made for some uncomfortable moments.

For instance, when I picked up the pictures I had printed for the photo board we'd display at the funeral, the cashier recognized Andy in the snapshots.

"How is she?" the cashier asked with concern, pointing to the woman in the photos with Andy.

"*She* is me," I replied, trying to smile through it. "I am her."

The lady looked at me, confused. "Oh," she finally said. "But it doesn't look like you. I thought maybe you were her sister."

"Nope," I said. "It's me. I'm Andy's wife. But you're right—I don't look the same. I haven't taken a shower in, like, a week!"

She laughed awkwardly. I couldn't get out of there fast enough.

That Friday, December 23, Andy's body was ready to be viewed. I wanted this to be a private moment for immediate family, before the commotion of the wake and funeral. Just Andy's brothers and parents joined the kids and me for this viewing. We entered the funeral home and were greeted kindly.

I was nervous about how Andy would look. I wanted to view him first. I didn't want the kids to be scared if the decomposition had rapidly progressed. I hadn't seen Andy since that Wednesday morning at the medical examiner's office.

The kids, of course, hadn't seen their daddy since that morning he went missing, nearly a month earlier. The morning he told my baby boy, Ike, that he would be back later to show him all the pictures he took at the lake. More than anything, I needed the kids to finally see their daddy. I couldn't imagine them not being able to see him and say goodbye after the long wait.

Thankfully, Andy looked relatively good. His lips were not as pink as they had been when I first saw him. They were starting to gray. You could see the makeup on his face. But I knew my kids would be able to see their daddy without it being uncomfortable.

Before I brought them in, though, I decided to take a few precious moments with just the two of us. Just Andy and me. Once again, I softly laid my head on his chest and began to sing "The Luckiest."

I remembered the day years ago when he popped in a Ben Folds CD as we were driving in his little red Saturn. He sang along as "The Luckiest" played. I instantly knew it was "our" song. I remembered our wedding day, when he looked into my eyes and sang this song as we danced. I remembered dancing to this song in our room on each of our anniversaries.

And now I will play and sing this song whenever I visit Andy at the cemetery on each of our anniversaries—until the day I can look in his eyes while he sings it to me again.

I could have spent the whole night there, just being with him. Now, I'm obviously a person of faith. I know Andy is always with me. I believe he was not in that body lying in the casket. That said, it was still the body I had married. The body that had cradled our newborn babies. The body I was supposed to grow old with. It was all I had left.

After a few moments, I gathered the kids to bring them into the viewing room. My empathetic Ike wanted to be around his dad as much as possible. He was so drawn to Andy's body. He was not afraid to touch, hug, and kiss his daddy. I had to tell Ike to not kiss Daddy too hard, because some of the makeup was starting to come off.

It was all too much for Grace, though. As her mother, I needed to push her to go in to talk to and to look at her dad. She was only able to enter the viewing room one time.

Andy's passing has made me realize how different the kids' personalities really are. I now know I have to approach each child differently and meet them where they are in their grief. To this day, for instance, I still always have to reach out to Grace, prodding her to talk about her dad and how she feels. It's something I will gladly do for my lifetime, if I have to.

Everyone got to have their moment alone with Andy. They needed it. Each had their own special relationship with

Andy, and they were all owed that private time. I remember my mother-in-law also speaking of how she couldn't stay away from Andy. She wanted to be with him every moment. And just like my son, she wanted to touch Andy's arms and be close to him.

Afterward, I went in one more time. I had this uncontrollable urge to be the last one to leave him before we all left for the evening.

Before the wake and funeral, we did manage to celebrate Christmas. Again, so many rallied behind me and my small children. Countless presents and gifts were donated to me, my children, and my unborn baby. The number of people I wanted to thank and later tried to thank felt overwhelming.

Despite the incredible outpouring, I basically sat through Christmas just trying to smile for the kids. I had always loved Christmas—I didn't want it to be forever changed for them. I wanted it to continue to be special.

For me, on the other hand, I'm not so sure Christmas will ever be the same. It will be *different*. That doesn't mean it can't be happy again too. But now it'll always be different. Just like my entire life. I think they call this the "new normal."

Barf.

After Christmas, the wake and funeral went off without a hitch. Funerals aren't fun to write about, and I'm quite certain they're not enjoyable reading material either. So let me just tell you—it was all a blur.

At the wake, there were so many people to hug. So many "I'm so sorrys." So many teary faces. I just needed to hold it together on autopilot.

We had tons of photo boards plus a slideshow with many other pictures of Andy with family and friends. I tried to include all aspects of his life, to show how loved and special he was to all of us.

Ike and Grace also made their own "Daddy boards" with wonderful pictures of just them and their daddy. They were his most important people. I wanted them to see that love in photos so they could always remember it. Those boards are now framed and displayed in their bedrooms.

Not to mention, there was also a display for our unborn baby, Sully. A special onesie was made for him that said "My daddy is special—God made him an angel."

We then had the funeral service the next day. During the visitation period before the service began, the church quickly filled with everyone I loved. People greeted me again, hugged me again, cried again.

It was touching to have the military present in so many ways. Flags covered Andy's casket and were held outside the door as people arrived. A military serviceman also stood next to Andy before the service began. It was very moving. Just how Andy would have wanted it.

My mind and body were on full autopilot now, even more than at the wake. If I had stopped to "feel," I knew I would surely break down and not get back up. (You know—the whole crying-on-the-bathroom-floor routine.)

But as much as I tried to numb myself, there was still a growing ache in my heart. Andy's casket was open during the visitation period. But once the service was ready to start, the casket would be shut. Our final goodbyes were quickly approaching.

Ike was once again drawn to his daddy's body. But Grace was still struggling. My motherly instincts were in overdrive as I encouraged this beautiful, strong-willed, 100 percent daddy's girl to look at and say goodbye to her father. The man she had wrapped around her little finger from the first moment he laid his hand on her chest and stopped her from crying.

She did say goodbye—and I am so glad she had that moment. I wanted no regrets for her. It was already enough to have lost her daddy; I didn't want her to be too afraid to say goodbye to him.

Once she said her goodbye, now all I could think about was my own. Any moment now, the casket would be closed.

Once again, I fully understood that his spirit was gone. But that body was all I had left in this physical world. It was more than a body. It was those eyes that could not stop looking at me in my dorm room when we first started dating. Those arms that held me so close and always protected me. Those lips that kissed me gently on the day he left for the lake. Those hands that always wiped away my tears and took away my worries. His body was my life.

And now it would be gone forever.

I would never be able to see this man again. I had just gotten him back from the lake, and now I would lose him again.

The moment arrived. It had to happen. There in the back of the church, we said our final goodbyes. I gave Andy a final kiss. I was the last to say goodbye.

Then the casket was shut. The wedding vow "till death do us part" rang terrifyingly in my head. It still brings shivers to my spine.

I held my baby girl's hand and scooped my six-year-old boy into my arms ever so gently, avoiding my baby bump that was now too hard to conceal. Together, we proceeded up the long church aisle, with Andy's best friends in the world bearing his casket behind us.

The ceremony was beautiful. But I couldn't make eye contact with anyone. I snuggled my babies close through the songs and readings. My uncle gave an inspiring and touching homily—so I have been told. I can't remember a word of it. It seemed fitting, though, for him to give Andy's final homily, as he was the one who married us.

As the service came to a close, "Ants Marching" was played, as promised. We processed down the aisle as a family of five—me, Andy, two kids, and one on the way—for the final time in my life. Just as I imagined, I could feel the angels and Andy above us dancing. It was the strangest moment of euphoric happiness and desperate sadness I will probably ever experience. I knew Andy was with us, yet he was so far, far away.

We rode out to the cemetery in the limousine donated by our loving community. We all gathered in the cold around the casket.

If you ever attend a military funeral where there will be a final roll call, "RUN! HOLY SHIT!" are the only words that come to mind.

For those of you who don't know what it is, let me explain. It's like a teacher calling attendance in a classroom. The very last name called is that of the deceased.

So one by one, they called out each name of the attending members of Andy's military company. Each member replied, "Here."

At the end, they yelled, "Stifter!"

Silence.

"Stifter!"

Earth-shattering silence.

"Stifter!"

Disgusting silence.

I could feel my knees buckle. I could not breathe or move or feel. My dad's arms wrapped around me to keep me from falling.

The burial service came to an end. As others headed back to their cars, I lingered. I wanted to be the last to touch the casket before this man I gave my life to was to be buried in the ground. I laid my hand on the casket one final time, then proceeded to the limo.

It had been a pattern since the private viewing on Friday—I always had to be the last to say goodbye. I had no regrets with our marriage. I would have none with his death. I knew I was fulfilling Andy's final wish as well. I knew I was the one he wanted at his final goodbye. I lived up to "till death do us part."

The luncheon followed the funeral. More people to greet and talk to. Andy always said, "Kate, I'm the brains, and you're the spokesmodel." But I didn't know *this* was what I signed up for.

That evening, the kids, my mom, and I went to dinner, then we took the kids swimming at the hotel where my aunt was staying. After swimming, we got ready to head back home. Ike and I waited in the lobby while Grace got a hot chocolate.

That was when my Ike looked up at me and said, "Mommy, I wish I could just hold Daddy's hand."

In my head, I started yelling at Andy, just as I would have if he had been next to me: "Andy, hold the boy's hand!"

As we walked out not but a minute later, Ike was holding his hand up in the air. I thought he wanted me to take his hand in mine, so I reached for it.

"No, Mom," he said so matter-of-factly. "I'm holding Daddy's hand."

My mouth dropped to the ground and shivers went piercing up my spine. "How do you know Daddy is holding your hand?" I asked.

"He told me he wanted to hold my hand," he once again said matter-of-factly.

Believe what you want. But I *know* my son was holding his daddy's hand at that moment.

We finally arrived home. It had been a long day. A long week. You get so caught up in funeral planning. But once it's over, you're left asking, *Now what?*

Life. That's what.

The hardest part is after the funeral. No one told me that. Now we had to start living our life without Andy. Now we had to start our new normal.

Again, barf.

Chapter 9

MY NEW TRIBE

OK, what do you do after your spouse's funeral? What did *I* do? What was I, as a pregnant widow with two other kids, even supposed to do?

Well, for two weeks, I basically watched TV and slept until the kids got home from school.

My work had given me time off, encouraging me to return whenever I was ready. But I wasn't ready. I knew if I went back, I would do nothing but cry. Plus, I would have to face everyone . . . ugh.

Don't get me wrong—I love all the people I work with. But in those days after the funeral, I just couldn't bear the thought of facing the looks and the "welcome backs." I was an extreme extrovert before Andy went missing. But I was still struggling with being around people. For the first time, I had to go on medication for my anxiety and depression.

In those two weeks after the funeral, I had the weight of an elephant on my chest. It just wouldn't go away. I had no relief. It felt as if my heart were literally breaking.

Now, I had lived through some painful breakups in the past, so I had experienced heartbreak. Actually, let me rephrase that—I *thought* I had experienced heartbreak. I don't mean to suggest that it doesn't hurt when you break up, because it does! But the death of your spouse is a totally new level of heartbreak.

This heartbreak means watching your future, the secure life that you know, get buried in a casket along with the love of your life. It means watching your babies sobbing for their daddy. It means watching your belly grow with a baby who would never know his father. It is . . . pure devastation.

You never truly recover from this heartbreak. Instead, you become a new you. But the silver lining is, *you* get to choose who the new you is.

Eventually, I knew I couldn't just sit at home and cry, sleep, and watch TV all day. If I continued to do that for an extended amount of time, it could get unhealthy. Plus, I knew I would need to take time off for maternity leave at the end of April. Not to mention, I realized I needed something to distract me from myself.

So, heigh-ho, heigh-ho, it's off to work I go.

I'd been dreading facing my coworkers, when in fact, everyone was wonderful when I returned. I could not ask for a better place to work or better people to work for and with. I am forever grateful to these people.

During this transition back, the local chapter leader of the Modern Widows Club (MWC) reached out to me with an invitation to attend their meetings. I had never heard of the MWC. It's a national organization, but the only Minnesota chapter is—lo and behold—right in Waconia. Weird.

What do I have to lose? I thought.

So, just six short weeks after Andy had died, I attended my first meeting. I was very nervous before I walked in that door. It ended up being one of the best decisions of my life.

When we think about widows, most people picture elderly women. But this group had young widows, just like me! Right in my own town!

They immediately embraced me. I felt life rush into me—someone understood my pain. It was almost as if God were saying, "Katie, you've had this tragedy, and I'm sorry. But I'm gonna have you meet these other women to help you on your journey."

At every meeting, we watch a video from the founder of the MWC. It's emotional and heartfelt. Each month brings a new topic on widowhood, from finances to finding your passion. That first time, I held my tears through the whole thing. Looking back, that was so silly. This was the place where tears and raw emotions were accepted and encouraged. This was a judgment-free zone.

One thing I've learned about my wisters (yep, widow sisters) is that they're the least judgmental, most accepting, and most loving people you'll ever meet. We're not a group to pity. We wouldn't wish our pain on our worst enemy, yet we do wish we could give you a glimpse of our life perspective. (If you stick around for chapter 12, you'll learn more about it.)

The point is, these were my people, my tribe.

Let me clarify something right here: your tribe is not the same as your support system of family and friends. I am forever indebted to my family and friends. And I know that they experience the grief, pain, and loss of Andy's death in their individual ways.

But they can't understand *my* loss. How could they? They've lost a son or son-in-law, a brother or brother-in-law, a friend, a coworker. But only I am his wife, the mother of his children. Only I am the widow, who lost the entire life she had planned with her husband.

But my widow tribe—they understand my loss exactly. They've lost their spouses in a variety of ways. Some recently, some years ago. Some have remarried, some haven't—or haven't yet. We all have a unique story, yes. But my loss is their loss. It's *our* loss.

From that first meeting, my wisters became my lifeline. It was like air reentering my lungs after not breathing for weeks. It made my journey feel normal, my feelings validated. It allowed me to feel complete acceptance.

These women understand that the true gift of widowhood is that we each choose how we carry the burden of our loss. Me, I carry it with the sarcastic, sick widow humor I've shared with you many times in this book. I carry it by laughing and making jokes about death that other people find uncomfortable. (We all need some fun in life, right?)

Honestly, though, there are also days when I try to pretend I'm not a widow, that this never happened to me, or that it could just magically "go away." More than anything, I want happiness again, to not feel alone.

The feeling of utter loneliness has been the worst part of this never-ending journey of widowhood. Sometimes this loneliness takes a physical form. It's an intense sensation, a heavy weight, that finds a home in my upper chest. It sits there as I try to catch my breath.

The loneliness can also cause my heart to race and sheer panic to set in. I experience the fight-or-flight response daily. Panic attacks have occurred. Sometimes I feel like I want to crawl out of my skin or hurt myself. Other times, my body feels like it's just floating through this life, with no sensations.

Wanting to hurt yourself or not live anymore are serious thoughts that need attention. Grief is a dark journey that can seem endless. You must find ways to cope—to give yourself reprieve from the desperation. Coping for me came in many forms: doctors, therapists, my tribe, and family. You are not alone in this, but you need to seek help.

My mind experiences the brunt of the loneliness, though. The day Andy disappeared, the first thing I said to Ann was, "I don't want to be alone." Staring at that paddleboard, the thought of losing Andy and living without him was my biggest fear. He was the love of my life. The man who danced around with a

Troll hat to make me laugh and who sang our wedding song to me each and every anniversary. We had a home. A life. We were raising small children with another one on the way.

I lived with that fear for three weeks and four days. And here I am, still facing it. I will always face it.

These fears are worst at night, though not in the way you might assume. I'm not talking about the fear of hearing strange noises and worrying about intruders when you're the only adult in the house. Truth be told, that type of thing did scare me back when Andy would travel out of town for work.

But now, a deeper fear grips me when the kids are in bed and darkness sets in. There on the couch or in my bed, I realize I am *alone*. My husband is dead. My dream for the future is dead. I'm terrified of being this woman alone in her house at night for the rest of her life.

I own this loneliness. There is nothing you or anyone can do to fix it. It's mine to deal with. But at least I know I'm not alone in this aloneness. My widow tribe understands what I'm going through.

More importantly, they also help me see there *is* a future for me. It's such a wonderful thing to know women in all different stages of grief. I look to them and see that life and love after grief are possible, if you let them happen!

This was exactly what I needed six weeks after Andy died: a ray of light in ultimate darkness. To this day, these women continue to be my light in my dark. I will forever be a member of the Modern Widows Club, even when (not "if" — I'm being optimistic) I remarry.

That's because I'll *always* be a widow. I'll *always* carry the burden of loss in my heart. A part of me will *always* belong to Andy. I'll never deny or hide that.

However, none of this will take away from the new love I'll find in my future husband. (Again, being optimistic.) I know this because I've witnessed it with my tribe and the new love they have found.

The heart is a very resilient thing. Just as it can experience pure devastation, it can mend and love again. No, it'll never be the same heart as before. The death of a spouse leaves scars. Just as we get laugh lines on our face from great joy, we get scars on our heart from great loss. And I would remove neither! The laugh lines and the scars represent the same thing: the love and joy we have experienced in life.

My scars are deep, but that's because I loved this man deeply. Even though our story ended in devastation, I would never change a moment. These scars allow me to love more deeply, embrace life more fully, and hold my loved ones even more closely. I've learned this from my widow tribe, and they are 100 percent correct.

I apologize if this chapter seems super rant-y and soapbox-y. But to sum it up, if you experience devastation, find a tribe. You are not alone—know that. There are always people who have gone through a similar experience.

Your job is to get out there and find them. Even if you don't feel up to it (and believe me—you won't), don't talk yourself out of it. If I had sat at home and cried all day, I wouldn't have found this widow group right in the town I live in. That doesn't mean you have to find a grief group, as I did. Just surround yourself with positive people with similar experiences who want to help.

Do it! Because you are *not* alone.

Chapter 10

The Parenting Widow

Let me be brutally honest: I hate widowed parenting.

I know that's a really brave thing to admit. I know someone might think that means I don't want or love my kids.

That could not be further from the truth.

I love my children with my whole heart. I would die for them. At times, they are the one and only reason I choose to live! They have kept me afloat when I was drowning. (Maybe that's a bad analogy. Remember? Spouse drowned?)

But I never wanted to be a widowed parent, to parent alone. I never wanted sole responsibility to make every decision and action—financial, spiritual, emotional, and practical— for my children. I never wanted sole responsibility for their safety and security. I never wanted sole responsibility for the endless whining. (Of course I had to add that—it's a big one!)

Most importantly, I never wanted to be the only one to witness all the love and joy of the children Andy and I made together. In chapter 9, remember when I said I'll always be a widow, even when I remarry? For the same reasons, I'll always be a widowed parent.

My future husband will be an important person in my children's lives and will love them too. But Andy—and only Andy—is their *father*. He is the only person who could truly love these children as much as I do. For every birthday party, wedding, lost tooth, and first bike ride, a part of me will always grieve in that moment, because he is not there. Andy was a beautiful soul who will always be missed as a husband and a father.

These thoughts weighed on me more and more with every passing day of my pregnancy. I kept thinking about how I would deliver a baby alone. Well, not *literally* alone. My mom and Ann planned to be there with me. But Andy—my baby's father, the only person I wanted to share this moment with— wouldn't be there.

So what did I do? How did I survive that beautiful moment without my husband?

I started by searching for others who had gone through the same experience. I loved my wonderful widow group, but no one had gone through pregnancy and birth without the father of her child.

Then I found Erica Roman in one of my online groups. Like me, she was a blogger. On her website at https://ericarom an.me/, she wrote a beautiful article about the birth of her son without her spouse. She compared the birth to her grief.

I finally didn't feel alone in my experience. To this day, I feel connected to her through our shared experience, even though we have never met. The words she wrote were so impactful that I need to quote them here, with her permission:

> *The rhythm of labor contractions mirrors the pain in the early stages of grief. Intense waves of pain followed by a time where you feel nothing. It's how I was able to speak at the funeral. I was in one of the stretches of numbness where I could function as if my whole world wasn't burning before my eyes.*
>
> *But when the pain came, even though it was emotional, it manifested physically as well. Just like labor contractions I could recognize their approach before I could feel their pain. It started somewhere deep within, twisting my insides with a monstrous grip. When I felt the beginning of this process I would promptly find a place where I could get through it in private. Some processes of life and death aren't meant to be experienced publicly.*
>
> *If I managed to escape somewhere (bathrooms seemed to be my go-to grief haven), I would succumb to the pain, letting it have its way with me until the wave passed. If escape wasn't possible I would find something to focus on. A light switch, a piece of food, a song on the radio. I would concentrate all of my mental energy on that one thing until there was nothing left to focus on the pain. I used the same method to get through my labor contractions.*

I clung to these words as I approached the day I would welcome my little boy. I reminded myself that others had done this, and so could I.

I scheduled an induction, which would ensure that my obstetrician—remember the hug from chapter 6?—would deliver my baby. I *needed* him there. His gentle kindness was what I needed most.

I officially began my maternity leave the day before I was scheduled to deliver. I had lunch with family and did a little shopping to keep my mind off the next day.

That night was probably my most challenging. I remember lying on my bed in the same position where Andy had last cuddled me the morning of his death. I just lay there sobbing, wishing Andy were with me and praying to God for help. Actually, "Help me" is a common phrase I use in prayer. There are moments when that's all I can muster. And God knows. He just knows.

The next morning, the craziness began. Mom, Ann, and I drove to the hospital. I checked in and got into my gown. There was a lot of excitement with waves of sadness.

In the back of my mind, I tried to push away the thought of "He isn't here." I wanted to replace that pain with the overwhelming joy I would feel as I met my new son. But that's a joy you want to experience with the father. Thus, I found myself in an emotional loop.

April, my nurse, entered. She had been specifically selected to be my nurse—an assignment she wholeheartedly agreed to take on. This labor and birth would be most definitely "different" than most. It would take a special person, and April was exactly what I needed. She was caring and compassionate, and she met my expectations a thousand times over. I will always remember her and be so grateful for her care. In fact, she told me that before she started work that day, she took time to pray for me and to pray that Andy would be with us throughout this process.

Remember when I said people are good? This was more than just "people are good." This was God talking and working through this woman, reminding me that he is always with me, even when my hope is gone and I feel I can't carry on.

As it turned out, this labor was the easiest of the three for me. It was virtually pain-free (with help from the epidural too).

Andy was there for sure. Throughout the day, the machines that monitored my IV, blood pressure, and contractions kept turning off and on. And the minute hand on the clock started speeding up out of nowhere.

Then there was the beautiful moment when my baby boy was placed on my chest. I remember it as if it were yesterday. I will remember it for the rest of my life.

I felt Andy's presence so strongly. *He was there.* There is not a question in my mind or heart. I felt him. It was as if we three—Andy, the baby, and I—were in our own bubble as we embraced this moment of new life.

After all, Andy never would have missed that moment, and he knew I never would have let him miss it. That's how we worked, and even death couldn't stop it.

After the birth, the parade of people came. The community that had rallied around me during the search and after Andy's death also rallied around me in my delivery room. It was loud and crazy, but I wouldn't have changed it for anything in the world. I needed those people at that moment.

It is strange, though, how you can be surrounded by joyful, happy, and loving people yet also feel utterly alone.

The parade eventually left, including Mom and Ann. They all promised to return the next morning.

Night approached. Loneliness set in. It did every night, of course. But this night was especially devastating.

That first night after a birth, it should be just you, the man you love, and the new child you created together. There in the darkened, quiet hospital room, you should be loving on each other and talking about the beautiful moment you brought your new baby into this world.

Andy and I shared that experience after the births of our other children. It meant so much to me. Before Andy died, it was what I had looked forward to the most.

Instead, I was alone with a new baby who would never meet his father. If you think women are emotional after birth, try a widow who just delivered a baby alone. Raw emotion is the only way I can describe it. Such a mix of pure happiness and pure sadness, lying in a hospital bed next to the most beautiful baby, who was peacefully sleeping.

This is widowed parenting.

Parenting alone is not something I signed up for. Suddenly finding myself widowed was hard enough, but parenting through it almost seemed like an impossible feat. I was not only responsible for my grief and healing but also for three little ones. It left me with thoughts of fear and loneliness—still does.

Not a day goes by that I don't question my parenting ability. Am I a good parent? Is that the right decision for my child? I just want them to be OK. I just want them to be happy. But it's completely exhausting.

Guilt takes the form of fear too. I still feel guilty that I couldn't protect my children from this pain. Seeing your children suffer is heartbreaking.

As a widowed parent, I hold my children's grief along with my own. I wonder, how will their dad's death impact their overall well-being? Am I seeing normal "kid" behavior, or is it grief shining through? I have constant worries and many sleepless nights thinking about what-ifs and the sad stories you hear about others whose lives turned to turmoil after losing a parent.

In fact, if I could just pluck all their grief from them and add it to my endless pile, I would in a heartbeat. But I can't. And knowing that I can't fix this problem for them is the hardest truth I've ever had to accept.

But I will take all the self-doubt, guilt, and fear any day over the loneliness of widowed parenting. Being alone in a house with my children day in and day out—without my Andy—is the deepest kind of loneliness I have ever felt.

There's no one to share all the joys the kids bring. No one to talk to about their report cards. No one to call me to see what's for dinner. No one to let me have a break when the kids are driving me crazy.

This is what I miss the most.

So if you're a widowed parent—or if you're raising a child or children on your own for *any* reason—repeat after me: *I will accept help.*

Say it again: *I will accept help.*

One more time, to make it stick: *I will accept help!*

It's time to let go of your pride. You are not less of a person—less of a mother or father or guardian—if you need help. In fact, you're *stronger* if you get the help you need.

At first, accepting help was really challenging for me. It felt strange to let others into my situation. To let them know how much I was hurting and how much of a mess I was.

But these are the moments when we need others more than anything. We need to let them in.

So take the damn help. The people in your support group know they can't take away your pain. But they *can* watch your kids, mow your yard, fix your sink, drive your kids to soccer, make you dinner, and do whatever you need to make life a little easier. This is especially true if you are grieving as well as parenting. Most people truly do want to help, so let them.

And to those of you who know a widowed parent or any parent doing it on their own, here's some advice: don't say "Call me if you need me." I've never called anyone who said that to me, even if they sincerely wanted to help.

Instead, be specific. Say, "Want me to take the kids to a movie tomorrow night?" or "Here's a pizza." Just show up and *do* something. (We'll discuss this more in chapter 11, because this isn't just a widowed parent issue. The same advice goes for helping anyone grieving, parent or not.)

Though it was difficult at first, I have learned to embrace help. I may be a solo parent, but I know I can't actually do it alone. I cannot be in twelve places at one time. Without help, my children couldn't participate in activities, which make them happy and healthy, and I couldn't get out of the house, which makes me happy and healthy too.

So accept help. And for the rest of you, if you see widowed or single parents struggling, reach out and help them. Remember, we live for others, for relationships.

We need each other.

Chapter 11

HOW TO HELP SOMEONE WHO IS GRIEVING

Yep, we've reached the how-to section of the book. If you know someone on a grief journey and want to help them along the way, this chapter is especially for you. That said, if you're on your own grief journey, don't think you can just skip ahead to chapter 12. This chapter is for you too—it can help you learn about the support you need and should be seeking out.

So how *do* you help those of us on a grief journey? After ten chapters, I hope you've taken note of the support I received from family, friends, professionals, and even strangers. I hope you've seen what helped me—and what didn't help me, no matter how well intended. So now I want to pull these ideas together in an easy-to-follow how-to.

Mind you, this is just my opinion. It's what helped me and what I've learned from listening to others who have experienced loss. But as I see it, supporting someone in grief is very simple: show up, be there, and pray for us.

That's it.

As obvious as these three things may seem, they might be quite difficult for some people. That's because most of us don't know how to deal with grief, whether it's our own or someone else's. Remember back in chapter 1, when we talked about how we need to break taboos about death and grief?

Let me be honest: before I lost Andy, I said and did the wrong things when people were grieving. And I was a trained school counselor. When working with students who had experienced loss, I talked about the stages of grief, how everyone grieves differently, how to remember your loved one, the importance of saying goodbye—and so on and so forth.

That type of support was all fine and necessary but very naive. It came from someone who hadn't yet experienced the true trauma of loss.

Now, I don't mean that grief is like some exclusive members-only club. You don't *have* to experience tremendous loss in order to know how to support others. In fact, I hope you never have to experience this type of loss.

What I mean is, until Andy's death, I had no idea what I was talking about when I spoke of grief. It took losing the love of my life, the father of my children, to fully understand that grief goes much, much deeper than most of us realize.

I hope you can come to some level of that same understanding without having to experience such loss yourself. It's one of the reasons I share my story in this book—so my experience can help you learn how to better support others.

So don't feel bad if you haven't been there for those of us who are grieving or if you've said or done the wrong thing. As I've said, I did too. But now you have the power to change. And I hope this how-to can help.

Let's start with being there—just simply being there. Maybe it's at the funeral, at a holiday gathering, or at Target as we're buying underwear because we're too overwhelmed to do laundry. (Remember that?) Maybe it's in the first few hours or a few years later.

You know how there's a time for *doing* and a time for *being*? Well, *being* there means just being present in whatever way we need you. I think of Romans 12:15: "Rejoice with those who rejoice, weep with those who weep."

In these moments of being, please let go of the notion that there's some "magical" thing you can say. Don't try to "fix" things or us with words.

In truth, I'd love to tell you, "Say *these* words, and everything will go away." But I can't. No words—not even "I love you" or "I'm here for you"—can make grief just go away. Grief doesn't go away, ever. I hope you're starting to understand that by now. It's not something to "fix" or "get over." We simply learn to carry it with us for the rest of our lives. Therein lies the beauty of loss.

So maybe the best thing to say—if you need to say anything at all—is this: "There are no words. But I'll sit with you and listen to whatever you want to talk about. I'll be your shoulder. I'll pray with you. I'll hold you while you cry."

Looking back, I don't remember any insightful words people thought they were telling me. I just remember them being there with me. Sitting with me while I cried. Answering the phone late at night when I couldn't sleep and just needed to reach out. Texting me or calling me daily, even if I didn't respond or pick up the phone. Their presence and their love and care helped me through it.

Simple, isn't it? Just be there. If you can't be there in the flesh, send a card in the mail, pick up the phone, send an email. We're well into the twenty-first century; there are plenty of ways to be present even when you're miles away.

Part of being there means setting aside your fear, as we discussed in chapter 1. In particular, don't let your fear keep you from talking about our loved one who has died. Don't let your fear make you shy away. Don't pretend this death didn't happen, because it did. And don't think for a second that you can't talk about our loved one because you're afraid it will make us "sad."

Part of being there means telling stories, laughing, reminiscing. Oh, how my children light up when others talk about their dad.

And yes, sharing stories can cause tears, but that's OK. If we cry or get sad because you say something, it only shows our love. There is no grief if you didn't first love. Crying, like laughing, is a normal human function, a release for our body. So talk about the dead as a wonderful way to continue their legacy and the love they had on this earth.

So let's move on now. The next step in the how-to is to show up. This is the *doing*.

During my most intense grief, something amazing happened. Food was brought to me. Maternity clothes showed up at my door. Christmas lights were hung on my house. Presents were wrapped. All these things I could not accomplish on my own were done for me—without me uttering one single word.

This is what I remember and appreciate the most. Having people show up took a huge level of responsibility off my plate—especially during those days when getting out of bed was a struggle.

As we discussed in chapter 10, don't say "Call me if you need me." We won't. Not because we don't need the help. But because we're just a *wee* bit busy trying to survive every minute of the day in the midst of deep grief. Exhaustion, sadness, and pride might just stop us from picking up the phone.

Instead, *you* need to call us. Just come right out and say you'll take the kids for the day or you're heading over with some takeout or you've arranged an outing.

Or don't even bother to call. Just show up to rake leaves, shovel the driveway, or take the dog for a walk. Leave a cooler outside the house so you and other sneaky elves can magically fill it with food at any time. Sometimes the greatest gift is the one that goes unnoticed.

Recently, I was out mowing my lawn—with help from my neighbor, who has to start the mower for me. I was having a crummy day, as loneliness was seeping in and taking over.

But then I suddenly noticed that someone had patched the holes a woodpecker had made in my siding. I instantly began to sob.

I didn't ask anyone to fix this. Someone just came over and did it. They didn't wait for me to call them. They didn't ask. They didn't even tell me that they had done it. It was such a small task, but in that moment, it meant the world to me. It meant so much more than that person will ever know.

That is how you help. That is how you *do*.

That is how you show up.

And once again, you need to push past your fear. Some people are afraid to call us or stop by. They worry it's a bother or that they're intruding. In my own experience, I've never felt intruded upon by someone helping me with my yard or stopping by with a meal. All of it was appreciated. So please, just take the leap, show up, and offer your help.

If you're worried about overstepping or offering the wrong kind of help, talk to one of our family members or close friends. They'll give you some great ideas. Or just come right out and ask us. Maybe we want help with our laundry. Or maybe we don't want you touching our unmentionables, thank you very much, so we'll show you where the vacuum is instead.

The thing about showing up is that you need to keep doing it. This isn't something you do in those first few days before and after the funeral, but then you're off the hook once you assume we're back on our feet.

Let me tell you: most people would never guess how much I struggle to this day. In the time since Andy's death, I've developed coping skills to help keep grief, panic, and sadness from taking over my whole day. Some days it works. Some days it doesn't. Anxiety and sadness will always be there, lurking, waiting to pull me back to their dark place. That's because I will always love and miss Andy.

So yes, eventually we'll be able to get out of bed, return to work, do most of the household chores, and seemingly look "normal" to you. But please remember this doesn't mean our grief is "over" and that you should stop helping us.

In the grand scheme of life, taking time to check in with a friend, send a text, make a call, or babysit their children is so minimal for you, but it means so much to us. This is especially true for those of us struggling to manage a family and home after losing our partner, as we discussed in chapter 10.

Keep showing up even if we're grinning and bearing it and telling you we're fine. This is why it's best to do, not ask.

My grief journey has helped me let go of the thing called pride. I take the help. I know I need it. I know it makes me happier. And I know that if I'm happy, then my children and family are happier.

I also know that this is what life is all about. To help others, to show love for others, to have an empathetic heart, and to give yourself for the good of others—this is God's plan for us. For all those who have helped me in any way, small or big, I am forever in your debt. In return, I am now meant to pay this debt by helping and loving others. It's that simple.

The Funny Thing about Grief

And on that note, here's the final how-to: pray for us. Don't just say, "I'll pray for you." That's nothing but a cliché. Rather, *actually* pray. You don't even need to tell us you're doing it. Just add us to your prayers.

Me, I'll take any additional prayers as they come. The trauma of my loss was tremendous. Prayers for me and my family helped me then and help me now in the daily battle of "making it."

I love when people come to me and say so sincerely, "We still think of you and your family all the time. We pray for you daily." It's such a gift to know that someone is still thinking and praying for me and my kids. It really means more than you know.

About one year after Andy's death, there was a knock at my door. It was the ambulance driver from the day Andy first went missing. If you remember from chapter 5, he came up to me that horrible night, embraced me, and asked if we could pray together.

As he stood at my door, I sensed he was nervous. "You probably don't know who I am . . ." he said.

"Of course I do, Dave!" I replied. "You're the ambulance driver who prayed with me. That moment, that night, meant so much to me. That powerful moment in prayer."

"I've driven down this street many times," he said, still a little shy, "but I wasn't sure which house was yours. Anyway, I just want to tell you that my wife and I have been praying for your family this whole time. I'm so happy to hear of your new little one."

I was overwhelmed by his kindness. "Can I give you a hug?" I asked.

We embraced.

The fact that he cared so much a year later makes me truly believe in the good of humanity. The night we prayed on that gravel road near the lake, we were strangers connecting on both a human and spiritual level. And we did the same thing in that moment on my front porch. It makes me surer than ever that God put us on this earth to serve both him and one another.

So this is why I ask you pray for us. Pray when we lose our loved one, and keep praying in the days that follow. The fact that you're still thinking about our grief and that you understand we're still struggling is so impactful.

Here's one way to think of the role you play: As we grievers are spinning and hurling in the storm of grief, there seems to be no end in sight. Your presence, your gesture big or small, your prayer is like a hand that reaches in and holds ours. And though your act does not stop the whirling, twisting, and breathless pain and destruction the grief storm brings, it does bring us warmth, love, and hope. It helps us begin to rebuild again. Little by little, we can heal our hearts with your help.

So please, please, *please* never underestimate the power of one small act of kindness.

Chapter 12

A WIDOW'S PERSPECTIVE: WE KNOW THE SECRET TO LIFE

———————

After a whole chapter of telling you how to help widows, here's one thing you *don't* have to do: feel sorry for us. Widows are the most compassionate, nonjudgmental group I have ever known. We're a little bit of crazy but a whole lot of awesome. We love harder than anyone and know firsthand the importance of love and relationships. In the end, love is all we have and need.

Most importantly, you don't need to pity us because we know the secret to life.

Actually, the secret to life is literally right in front of everyone's eyes, but most people are blinded by the world. Well, we widows have had our eyes opened. We live with the widow's perspective. A perspective we wish we never would have gained through such tremendous loss. But we did, and we embrace it.

We want others to share our life perspective without having to experience our pain. So please allow me to share the widow's perspective with you now.

The secret to life is to live each day knowing it could be your last.

For starters, we don't fear death nor deny it. As we discussed in chapter 2, there's such a taboo about death in our society. Most people try to look young and hide from death for as long as possible. They pretend it's something that happens only to other people—not to them, not to their loved ones.

Sorry, folks. That's not how the world works. People *die*! That's not harsh; it's just truth. Death is inevitable. Every single person will experience loss and ultimately die themselves.

We widows accept this truth, because we've experienced it firsthand. But this knowledge gives us reason to live each day knowing it could be our last. It's a bittersweet gift that allows us to approach life in a whole new way.

We widows also know that even when death takes someone from us, our life must move forward. I get "stuck" sometimes, of course. This loss is tremendous. Earth-shattering. As with depression, grief puts you in a haze. At times you can't even see your hand in front of you. But I refuse to let self-pity drag me down. I know I must embrace my life as it is—I must live it.

At the same time, we understand that life moves forward for those around us. Yes, grief can be a very self-absorbed feeling. But just because we've experienced loss doesn't mean we don't want to be a good friend or family member. You are there for us. We want to be there for you.

For instance, I still want to hear about your vacation adventures with your husband. (I enjoyed vacations with mine too.) I still want to hear how your spouse is driving you crazy. (Mine did too.)

You don't have to hide your triumphs and pains, worrying you'll make us feel sad or make yourself look ungrateful. We don't want you to feel guilty that you still have your spouse— and sometimes still get mad at him—just because we don't have ours.

This is a good time to clarify something about the secret of life: living each day as if it could be your last doesn't mean being perfect and all sunshine-and-lollipops all the time. By no means am I perfect. (Many can testify on my behalf.) I still yell at my kids. They still drive me crazy. I still get upset and lose my temper. I still do many of the things I wasn't proud of in my former life, before I lost Andy.

But what I can tell you is that the widow's perspective helps me rise above all this. I forgive more easily. I'm kinder. I'm less judgmental. I'm very quick to apologize and admit my wrongdoing. (Andy would never believe that one.) I refuse to have enemies, hold grudges, or treat others with disrespect. I try to help people. And most importantly, I try to live each day with a loving heart.

Part of living each day as if it could be your last means choosing who is in your life. Surround yourself with positivity. Positivity breeds positivity; negativity breeds negativity. If someone is negative, set them free. Don't let naysayers bring you down.

I don't know about you, but I don't want to spend what could be my last day constantly being negative. The only person it hurts is me.

Actually, that's not true. Negativity also hurts those around you, especially if you have little ones. Don't breed negativity in your children. Find the positives in every day. Share that with others.

As we near the end of the chapter, I want to leave you with a Bible verse I find so meaningful from the widow's perspective: "'For I know the plans I have for you,' declares the Lord, 'plans to prosper you and not to harm you, plans to give you hope and a future'" (Jeremiah 29:11).

I know God was and is still with me on my grief journey. But I'll be honest: my greatest sin (I can't think of another word for it) is that I haven't always trusted whether God has a plan for me. Out of fear, I've tried to take life into my own hands, especially before I truly understood the widow's perspective.

This is why I leave you with that Bible verse. God *does* have plans for us. Now, this doesn't mean we should sit back and let life pass us by. No way! That's not what the secret to life is about. We still need to seek God, ask him what his plan is for us, and then embrace it with everything we've got. We need to live out God's plan for as long as we can, until he calls us to him.

Let me tell you: God's plan definitely turned out to be different than my plan. Having Andy and getting to grow old with him—that was my plan. Therein lies the problem. *My* plan. But I guess that's not my story and not how my life is supposed to work.

The thought that life should follow my plan is so insane. We as humans think we have control. That we don't need God. That is so far from the truth. Life is nothing without God. I cling to that truth even more now.

My life is unfolding according to God's plan, but that doesn't mean he chose for or caused Andy to die. Did God know it would happen? Yes. Did he prevent it? No. We have free will. Was it a punishment to me, my children, or Andy? No way! Andy simply chose to go paddleboarding that day; our lives are forever changed because of it.

When I am sad, when I feel as if I have no reason to live, when my life has been completely flipped on its ass and I'm in my darkest moment—this is when I realize my life is not mine to plan. I need to live this life for my Lord, and I need to live each day as if it could be my last. Then and only then will I have true joy and happiness.

The part of this verse that speaks to me the most is that God has plans for us to "prosper" and that there will be "hope and a future."

A future.

Those two words give so much hope to my heart. When Andy died, I learned to give up all control and put my life in my God's hands. I now know I'm not in control. But I trust that I will have *a future*!

I don't know what that future has in store for me. I will forever be in search of my new path. And as a widow who understands how suddenly death can come knocking at the door, I don't know how long of a future I will even have.

But I do know I will not stop living! I live for Andy. I live for my children. I live for me.

But most importantly, I live for the Lord. He and only he can give me a future, whatever that brings: a new husband, more children, a new home, a new career path. I am up for the adventure. To quote my love's most favorite band, "Life is short but sweet for certain."

I got the best of my Andy, and even though his death caused tremendous pain, I wouldn't trade it for the world! Because to grieve is to have loved deeply. Grief has made me the new person I am today. The person who loves deeply, looks to the future with hope, and knows the secret to life.

That is the widow's perspective.

Epilogue

How Am I Doing?

As I reflect back on the past few years without Andy, I'm still not sure how I did it or keep doing it. It still hits me—the realization that this is my new life, that the old me is gone, and that I am now trying to pick up the pieces and figure out a life without my spouse.

There are tough days and downright awful days. They may not occur every day as they did in the first year, but they are still there. They can still knock me off my feet out of nowhere. All in all, though, the normal days outnumber the bad. There are many happy days. There is hope for a future.

I hate the saying "Time heals all wounds," but there's some truth to it. Really, though, what heals (or doesn't heal) is what you do with your time after a loss. I've spent my time seeking a new life, new joy and happiness, a new normal. That has meant making changes, trying new things, seeking new relationships, accepting help, trying to move forward as best I can—basically, accepting life without Andy.

Grief and loss awareness have become passionate topics for me. I feel my mission is to share my story and help educate others regarding grief and loss. Hence, this book. I've also spent the past year speaking locally at different venues about my story and grief. We all experience loss in our lifetime, and I feel called to help others not feel alone in their journey.

Along with speaking and writing this book, I've been blogging my journey and sharing my story. I chose the pen name "The Wicked Widow," which my dad automatically thought was inappropriate. Actually, it's just a nod to one of Andy's favorite movies, *Good Will Hunting*. The movie was set in Boston, with their cool, unique way of talking. Me, I am *wicked* funny, *wicked* smart. Or at least I think I am.

I believe my children are happy. We continue to talk about their dad daily. We stay involved with friends, activities, church, and life in general. Birthdays, Christmas, Easter, weddings, Father's Day, graduations—these celebrations always bring a twinge of sadness, but they also bring a smile only Andy could give us.

In particular, Andy's birthday, Father's Day, and the anniversary of his passing are always celebrated. I want to make it special for the kids. I want to celebrate the love, laughter, and memories of their father. We took a child's dream trip to Disney World on the first anniversary of his passing. On his other special days, we make things for him, play music, and sing. Once we even set off fireworks on his grave—then ran because I was afraid the police might come.

Andy's second birthday post-loss has particularly special memories for me. We jammed to Dave Matthews Band as we painted rock ladybugs to place on his grave.

Many people believe their lost loved ones show signs to their family members. Ours are ladybugs. We still find them all over the house, even in the dead of winter. I'll be sad, and then as if by magic, one will be crawling on my bathroom window.

Before I go any further, I want to clarify two points: 1) I do keep a clean home; it is not infested with bugs. And 2) I do not believe my husband *is* a ladybug. (I'm not *that* crazy.) But I do think he shows himself to us and lets us know he's always around through ladybugs and other signs. My daughter often tells me in her sarcastic fashion, "Oh, Mom—look! A feather or a speck of dust or that random bird—it's Dad!" She does think I'm crazy!

Anyway, as we were leaving the cemetery on Andy's second birthday post-loss, my sweet little boy, who is now a third grader, asked if he could speak with Daddy alone. He was starting to sob at this point.

Words cannot describe the depth of sadness, the loss, the extreme pain I felt watching my seven-year-old crouching down, desperately sobbing, talking to his daddy. I remember thinking, *How am I actually getting through this? How many others could survive this?* It was both horrific and sweet wrapped up in a bow. It's my reality now. Bringing my children to visit their daddy means going to the cemetery now.

I later asked my baby boy, "What did you say to Daddy?"

He replied, "I told him, 'We brought you these ladybugs for your birthday, I love you, and miss you.'"

I will never forget that moment.

Now let's get to the good stuff. I know you're wondering if I'm in a new relationship. Yes, I have found a special person. (He actually took the picture for the cover of this book.)

He's wonderful. He fully accepts my grief and lets me talk about it. He doesn't feel jealous of my relationship with Andy. He knows that I will always love Andy and that I will always talk about him. He knows that my love for Andy does not reduce my love for him. In fact, he has this wicked joke that he'll get the next forty-plus years with me on earth, but in the afterlife, he'll be toast.

He loves my children. He knows the role he's stepping into with my children, who don't have a father. And he steps into it without question. He not only accepts it but embraces it.

I can say with 100 percent certainty that Andy had his hands in finding this man for me. I feel so lucky to be loved by Andy and now to love and be loved by Ryan.

Grief is a forever thing. We grieve because we loved. (I didn't come up with that—I'm sure I read it on Pinterest.) We will always grieve for Andy because of how much we loved him and still love him. Andy is not replaceable. We are the face of grief and what it looks like to live with loss. It's not pretty. It doesn't go away with time. There will always be a void. (So don't let anyone give you grief about your grief, no matter how long it's been since the loss. Seriously, people—stop the "Haven't you gotten over it yet?" stuff.)

Remember all those wonderful people I mentioned throughout the book? My family, friends, and tribe are still with me every step of the way. Through them, memories of Andy are always close by. They bring both joy and sadness.

So, how *am* I doing? My answer to that is, I am surviving. I know I'll see Andy again, and that will be such an unexplainable moment. I don't fear death as I used to. I have joy. I have sadness. I have new love. Most importantly, I'm living for Andy.

And I am still laughing.

This was for you, Bubby! I love you!

Acknowledgments

I would not have survived this journey had it not been for several special people. I have already spoken of and thanked many of you throughout this book, but I'd like to offer my appreciation here again.

To my children: You have given me a want and need to tell our story. Because of you, I also want to help educate others so their world will be more open to conversations about loss and so they will never feel alone in their grief.

To my mom and dad: You are the definition of unconditional love! You raised me in faith and love and would move the heavens and earth to help me!

To my mother-in-law: You dropped everything to support me—especially during those countless hours when you helped with the kids so I could write!

To my brothers, Chris and Andy, and their families: Thank you for taking care of your baby sister and my children.

To my brothers-in-law, Dustin and Tommy: Thank you for showing up and sharing your love for and memories of Andy with my children!

To my neighbor and best friend, Ann: For the late-night calls, tears, laughter, honesty, and so much more—I am truly grateful to have you right in my backyard!

To my tribe, including my father-in-law, friends, family, coworkers, and wisters: Thank you for all your love, support, and help. You have made an impact and helped move me forward in my grief!

To my Beaver's Pond family: Thank you for making it possible to do something I never thought I would do in my life. Project manager Laurie Herrmann, designer Dan Pitts, editor Angela Wiechmann, and proofreaders Lauren Hovde and Caitlin Fultz—thank you for letting me keep my voice and share my story through the publishing process.

Finally, to Ryan: Thank you for loving me for the woman I have become through my grief journey, for loving my children, for showing me that love after loss is possible, for supporting and encouraging me to keep writing and sharing my story, and for saying Andy's name with me!

About the Author

———

Katie Stifter is a widow, mother, high-school counselor, and sometimes-funny wannabe blogger raising three children solo. Laughter and humor have always been her jam, and she uses it in many ways to heal and live after loss. She hopes her story, thoughts, feelings, and ramblings will help you heal from your tragedy.

You can follow Katie on Facebook (@katiethewickedwidow), on Instagram (@katiethewickedwidow), or on her blog (www.thewickedwidow.com).

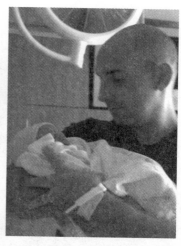